Letters:
Our American Story

Letters:
Our American Story

ANN BRUBAKER GREENLEAF WIRTZ

*Mayflower Granddaughter
and First Cousin to Benjamin Franklin*

RESOURCE *Publications* • Eugene, Oregon

LETTERS: OUR AMERICAN STORY

Copyright © 2025 Ann Brubaker Greenleaf Wirtz. All rights reserved. Except for brief quotations in critical publications or reviews, no part of this book may be reproduced in any manner without prior written permission from the publisher. Write: Permissions, Wipf and Stock Publishers, 199 W. 8th Ave., Suite 3, Eugene, OR 97401.

Resource Publications
An Imprint of Wipf and Stock Publishers
199 W. 8th Ave., Suite 3
Eugene, OR 97401

www.wipfandstock.com

PAPERBACK ISBN: 979-8-3852-5518-4
HARDCOVER ISBN: 979-8-3852-5519-1
EBOOK ISBN: 979-8-3852-5520-7

10/17/25

For
Inspirational
Letters
and
Connections to
American History,
Our gratitude is immeasurable.

Thanks be to God
for his great kindness,
and for the
Gifts of Mercy and Grace
received
through his Son Jesus Christ.

Fill your paper with the breathings of your heart.
—William Wordsworth, April 29, 1812
Letter to his wife, Mary

Contents

Permissions	xi
Connections: Key Historic Individuals and Family Groups	xiii
Family Groups and their Relationship to the Author	xvii
Understanding Genealogical Relationships and Terms	xix
Acknowledgments	xxi
How This Book Came to Be	xxv

JANUARY

Chapter 1: Genealogy Connects	3
Chapter 2: Women's Suffrage	7
Letter Envelope ~ Susan B. Anthony	13
Letter ~ Susan B. Anthony, 1903	14
Chapter 3: A Father and His Son	17
Letter ~ William E. Greenleaf, 1960	21
Chapter 4: Loss and Hope	24
Letter ~ Arie E. Greenleaf, 1963	27

FEBRUARY

Chapter 5: Teenage Inspiration	33
Letter ~ Ann Brubaker, 1964	37
Chapter 6: A Gracious Reply	39
Letter ~ Catherine Marshall, 1964	41

CONTENTS

MARCH

Chapter 7: A Mother's Heart	45
Letter ~ Mary Vanderhorst Greenleaf, 1960	47
Memoir ~ Mary Vanderhorst Greenleaf, 1976	49
Chapter 8: Ever Forward	51
Letter ~ Mary Vanderhorst Greenleaf Campen, 1976	53

APRIL

Chapter 9: A Heritage of Faith	59
Postcard ~ Arie Todd Greenleaf, 1997	62
Poem ~ Great-Grandfather Noah Brubaker, 1994	63
Chapter 10: A Gift Received	65
Letter ~ Irene Turner Wray, 2008	69
Letter ~ Irene Turner Wray, 2011	70
Letter ~ Arthena Wray Brubaker, 2011	72

MAY

Chapter 11: A Loving Son	75
Inscription ~ Arie Todd Greenleaf, 1993	80
Chapter 12: A Soldier's Story	81
Letter ~ Kenneth L. Brubaker, 1945	87

JUNE

Chapter 13: Math and the Space Race	95
Letter ~ Winston Ragon, 1972	100
Chapter 14: Good Friends	102
Chapter 15: The President Kennedy Era	106
A Peace Corps Reminiscence ~ Gail Monroe Crosson, 2025	110
Chapter 16: Television Tells a Story	112
Reunion Booklets, 1976 and 1986	118

CONTENTS

Chapter 17: Too Soon an Ending	120
Letter ~ Carol Shankland Kennedy, 1976	125

JULY

Chapter 18: A Southern Heritage	131
Chapter 19: Heading West	139
Letter ~ Frances Webber Brubaker, 1967	144

AUGUST

Chapter 20: A New England Heritage	146
Letter ~ Charlotte Remick Brubaker, 1972	152

SEPTEMBER

Chapter 21: Marriage, Birth, and Friendships	155
Letter ~ Jane Romack, 2014	161

OCTOBER

Chapter 22: Between the Lines	165
Letter ~ William Eugene Greenleaf, 1972	171

NOVEMBER

Chapter 23: The Gift of Encouragement	175
Postcard ~ Elisabeth Elliot, 1998	180

DECEMBER

Chapter 24: Building Memories	185
Letter ~ Carolyn Greenleaf Potterville, 2018	188
Letter ~ Laurie Opperman Greenleaf, 1979	189
Chapter 25: Grandchildren, Our Joy	190
Letter and Poem ~ Divya Greenleaf, 2024	194

CONTENTS

Letter Closings: A Benediction   196
How This Book Was Accomplished   198
Bibliography   201

Permissions

Scriptures marked AMP are taken from the AMPLIFIED BIBLE (AMP): Scripture taken from the AMPLIFIED® BIBLE, Copyright © 1954, 1958, 1962, 1964, 1965, 1987 by the Lockman Foundation Used by Permission. (www.Lockman.org).

Scriptures marked ESV are taken from THE HOLY BIBLE, ENGLISH STANDARD VERSION (ESV): Scriptures taken from THE HOLY BIBLE, ENGLISH STANDARD VERSION ® Copyright© 2001 by Crossway, a publishing ministry of Good News Publishers. Used by permission.

Scriptures marked KJV are taken from the KING JAMES VERSION (KJV): KING JAMES VERSION, public domain.

Scriptures marked NAS are taken from the NEW AMERICAN STANDARD (NAS): Scripture taken from the NEW AMERICAN STANDARD BIBLE®, copyright© 1960, 1962, 1963, 1968, 1971, 1972, 1973, 1975, 1977, 1995 by The Lockman Foundation. Used by permission.

Scriptures marked NIV are taken from the NEW INTERNATIONAL VERSION (NIV): Scripture taken from THE HOLY BIBLE, NEW INTERNATIONAL VERSION ®. Copyright© 1973, 1978, 1984, 2011 by Biblica, Inc.™. Used by permission of Zondervan.

Scriptures marked NKJV are taken from the NEW KING JAMES VERSION (NKJV): Scripture taken from the NEW KING JAMES VERSION®. Copyright© 1982 by Thomas Nelson, Inc. Used by permission. All rights reserved.

Scriptures marked NLT are taken from the HOLY BIBLE, NEW LIVING TRANSLATION (NLT): Scriptures taken from the HOLY BIBLE, NEW LIVING TRANSLATION, Copyright© 1996, 2004, 2007 by Tyndale House Foundation. Used by permission of Tyndale House Publishers, Inc., Carol Stream, Illinois 60188. All rights reserved. Used by permission.

Connections

Key Historic Individuals and Family Groups

KEY HISTORIC AND NOTEWORTHY INDIVIDUALS CONNECTED OR RELATED TO THE AUTHOR: ANN BRUBAKER GREENLEAF WIRTZ

Susan B. Anthony (1820–1906): Women's Suffrage; Letter addressed to Annie Pillsbury Young and to the organization founded by author's Great-Grandmother. Chapters 1, 2

Mary Perkins Bradbury (1615–1700): Salem Witch Trials; Eighth Great-Grandmother. Chapter 20

Phyllis Diller (1917-2012): Famous comedian; Daughter is high school friend. Chapter 14

T. S. Eliot (1888–1965): Nobel Prize Winning Poet; Seventh Cousin two times removed to Arie E. Greenleaf. Chapter 25

Elisabeth Elliot (1926–2015): Inspirational Author; Letters exchanged. Chapter 23

Jonathan Evans (1739–1806): Commander of Minute Men at the Lexington Alarm, April 19, 1775, Lexington, Massachusetts, the first battle of the Revolutionary War; Fourth Great-Grandfather. Chapter 18

Peter Folger (1617–1690): Missionary to the Wampanoag Indians on Martha's Vineyard and Nantucket, Massachusetts; worked with *Rev. Thomas Mayhew Jr. (1620/21–1657, ninth great-grandfather)* to learn their language and translate the first Bible in North America, *Up-Biblum* (1663) coordinated and completed by John Eliot at Harvard's Indian College (Fisher, *Peter Folger and Up-Biblum*, 2018); Eighth Great-Grandfather. *Chapter 18*

Peter Folger (1617–1690) *and Mary Morrell* (1620–1704): Eighth Great-Grandparents; Grandparents to Benjamin Franklin. *Chapter 18*

Benjamin Franklin (1705–1790): Founding Father, Revolutionary War Statesman & Diplomat, Signer of the Declaration of Independence, Inventor, Publisher; First Cousin eight times removed. *Chapters 5, 18*

Simon Greenleaf (1783–1853): Harvard "Royal Professor of Law," 1833; author, *Treatise on the Law of Evidence*; President of the Massachusetts Bible Society. First cousin five times removed to Arie E. Greenleaf. *Chapter 22*

Langston Hughes (1901–1967): Poet, Playwright, Activist, leader of Harlem Renaissance; Cousins through famous English Poet, Francis Quarles (1592–1644). *Chapter 25*

Nellie Kedzie Jones (1858–1956): Professor; leader in the field of Home Economics; developed Domestic Science Programs and Departments at (now) Kansas State University, Bradley University, University of Wisconsin; Grandmother graduated from a Nellie Kedzie program with a degree in Domestic Science from Kansas State Agricultural College, 1897. *Chapter 2*

Rev. Dr. Peter Marshall (1902–1949): Minister, New York Avenue Presbyterian Church, Washington, DC; Chaplain of the U. S. Senate; Biography: *A Man Called Peter*. *Chapters 5, 6*

Catherine Marshall (1914–1983): Inspirational Author; *A Man Called Peter*; Letters exchanged. *Chapters 5, 6*

Thomas Mayhew Sr. (1593–1682): First Governor of Martha's Vineyard, Massachusetts; Tenth Great-Grandfather; Father to *Thomas Mayhew Jr.* *Chapter 18*

Francis Quarles (1592–1644): English Poet: *Emblems, A Feast for Wormes*; Ninth Great-Grandfather. *Chapter 25*

Enoch Remick (1730–1800): Ancestor of Remick Country Doctor Museum and Farm, Tamworth, New Hampshire; Fourth Great-Grandfather. *Chapter 20*

Alan Shepard (1923–1998): Astronaut, first American in Space; Ninth Cousin. *Chapter 13*

CONNECTIONS

Richard Warren (Abt. 1578–1628): Mayflower Passenger, Ninth Great-Grandfather. *Chapter 20*

John Greenleaf Whittier (1807–1892): Famous American Poet; first-cousin nine times removed to Arie E. Greenleaf. *Chapter 22*

Every effort for accuracy has been made through extensive research, study, and evaluation.

Forgive any unintentional errors which may have occurred.

Family Groups
and their Relationship to the Author

BRUBAKER:

Noah: Great-Grandfather
Elizabeth (Baird): Great-Grandmother
Richard: Grandfather
Frances (Webber): Grandmother
Kenneth Lee: Father
Charlotte (Remick): Mother
Ken Jr.: Brother
Peter: Brother
Donald and Arthena (Wray): Second Cousins
Joel and Lorraine (Eller): Second Cousins
Irene (Turner) Wray (Brubaker descendant): Second Cousin

WEBBER:

George Martin: Great-Grandfather
Mariah Jane (Combs): Great-Grandmother

REMICK:

Benjamin Luce: Grandfather
Harriet (Vandivert): Grandmother

FAMILY GROUPS

VANDIVERT:

Robert Henry: Great-Grandfather
Mary Ursula (Kessler): Great-Grandmother

GREENLEAF:

Arie Eugene: First Husband
Arie Todd: Son (Dewa Shrestha)
Divya Aleydis: Granddaughter
Arie Aarush: Grandson
William Eugene: Father-in-law
Mary (Vanderhorst): Mother-in-law (W. E. Greenleaf, Robert Campen)
Clara Carolyn "Carol": Sister-in-law (George Fell, Butch Potterville)
Bill: Brother-in-law (Bobbie Jo Sauer, Virginia "Ginny" Garnsey)
Mary Margaret: Sister-in-law (Ken Palmer)
Daniel: Brother-in-law (Laurie Opperman)

WIRTZ:

William Patrick: Second Husband
Jack: Father-in-law
Helen (Patrick): Mother-in-law

Understanding Genealogical Relationships and Terms

Genealogical research establishes our connection to others based on determining the nearest Common Ancestor. This means finding out which Grandparent, or Great-Grandparent, or however far back one must go, is shared between individuals. There are charts available to calculate the family relationship.

First Cousins share the SAME GRANDPARENT(S) as their nearest Common Ancestor(s). This is the *foundational principle*.

Second Cousins share the same Great-Grandparents.

Third Cousins share the same Great-Great-Grandparents, and on it goes.

"Once removed," written 1x Removed, means there is one generation difference. "Twice removed," written 2x Removed, means there is a difference of two generations. *For example:*

The *child of a second cousin* is one generation removed from the Great-Grandparents.

The relationship between that child and one of the second cousins is described:

"Second cousins once removed," indicating the generational difference.

These two people have DIFFERENT GRANDPARENTS.

Their parents are not siblings. Their Common Ancestor is the person who is the Grandparent of one and the Great-Grandparent of the other.

When people have the SAME GRANDPARENTS but are in different generations, the number of times removed indicates the number of generations that have passed between them.

As first cousins, they represent *parallel lines of descent* through siblings.

Acknowledgments

THE SCOPE OF RESEARCH needed for this book and the months of writing necessary to complete the manuscript required a determined commitment to see it through. This could not have happened without the continuous support of family and friends.

I'm eternally grateful to my dear husband, Patrick Wirtz, who patiently answered every computer question and helped me through every conundrum. His love and prayers are constant and affirming. My dear son, Arie Todd Greenleaf, and his precious family, Dewa Shrestha Greenleaf, and their children Divya and Aarush, my beautiful grands, are always generous in their excitement, thrilled by all the family discoveries, and are the main reason for this work. It represents their heritage. Deep thanks to them for permission to include their writings in this book.

Weavers of Words (WOW), my writer's group, began in 2010. It is an accomplished and wonderful group of women. While our meetings are only occasional now, we remain a heartening source of encouragement and information for each other, which kept this project moving forward when doubts occurred. I'm forever in awe of my dear friends: Carol Guthrie Heilman, Sunny Lockwood, Leanna Sain, Betsy Thorne, and Karin Wooten.

It is a special honor to be allowed to include letters from two women who have uplifted the world with their lives and stories of faith. Nancy LeSourd has given permission to include a treasured letter by Catherine Marshall LeSourd which I received in response to my appreciation for her book *A Man Called Peter* (1951). Valerie Elliot Shepard has given permission to include an inspiring and heartfelt postcard received from her mother, Elisabeth Elliot, for a letter I sent conveying my love for her writings. These two letters are a blessing. Thank you, Nancy and Valerie.

I am deeply grateful to my loved ones who gave permission to publish the letters from our Brubaker families. To my brothers Ken and Peter, and

ACKNOWLEDGMENTS

to our Brubaker second cousins from Kansas, we are the inheritors of a tremendous legacy. Thank you for permission to share the beautiful and eloquent messages written by our mothers. Our ancestors lived a notable history, and one of the most significant accounts was written by Kenneth L. Brubaker Sr. Our father tells a portion of the World War II story, and Ken, Peter, and I are honored to share his valuable letter. It stands as a testimony of victory over evil.

Marrying into the Greenleaf family has been a gift for which I have everlasting gratitude. This book reveals a profound heritage of deep thought and insight which is still impacting generations today. We are extremely proud of this remarkable ancestry. I'm thankful for the family's permission to include letters from our late sister, Carol, and parents, William Eugene and Mary Vanderhorst Greenleaf. Our father's letters are illuminating and written with such astonishing sensitivity, I have chosen three to share. Mary's letters are also touching, and excerpts from her delightful memoir reveal some of the challenges of their first year of marriage in 1938. Her heartwarming tale demonstrates how love and faith are the underpinnings of joy despite our circumstances.

I sincerely thank Gail Crosson for penning a wonderful remembrance of her years serving in the Peace Corps in Brazil. She has written a fascinating narrative that evokes awe and wonder for all she did. Her story portrays a time when our country was on the cusp of change and is a jewel to share.

For my dear friends who gave permission to publish their personal messages and letters, a deep thank you is given. Your thoughts touched my heart then, and now. The letters were kept all these years because you beautifully convey the emotions of our common experience.

All who wrote the meaningful offerings in *Letters: Our American Story* were simply living their lives, the ups and the downs. They could never have imagined their words would come forth and impact anyone beyond the person(s) receiving their letter. This is a great responsibility, for I'm sharing the hearts and souls of those I cherish. It's very humbling. My profound thanks to everyone involved in this endeavor through your permission to publish these writings. Your agreement will allow others a greater understanding of our American story and the faith that undergirds our nation's history. God bless you.

My final thank you goes in two directions. To all the dearest ones who have been encouragers and prayer partners in this massive undertaking, this book reflects your faithfulness. I would name each of you individually, but I know someone would be overlooked. Please know your name is in my heart. Thank you.

The Lord's hand is evident upon this work. He directs my thoughts and pursuits every day and has revealed insights and ancestry that have made this book a reality. The depth of my gratitude is beyond expression, except to say: To God be the Glory!

> And whatever you do in word or deed, do all in the name of the Lord Jesus, giving thanks to God the Father through Him.
> Colossians 3:17 NKJV

How This Book Came to Be

We treasure our connection to the American story, our family heritage the identity that places us within the chapters of our national existence. Letters confirm who we are. They demonstrate the relationships we have with each other and the history that established our country. They are relatable through the sharing of common experience and thought. Our written expressions offer encouragement, gratitude, and love. Sometimes, they possess an archival significance that makes them extraordinary.

I am fortunate to have just such letters. Spanning over a century, they include a nostalgically hopeful letter by Susan B. Anthony, and a riveting WWII account written by my father, Kenneth L. Brubaker Sr. Both are revered for the inspiration and insight they convey and for the American history and humanity they tell. Their valuable contribution to our country's written record is the initial reason for *Letters: Our American Story*, but all the letters and messages represent moments in time when thoughts, emotions, and experiences were penned. Each is humbly and gratefully shared as a window into American history and into your own American story.

Ann Brubaker Greenleaf Wirtz
April 25, 2025

JANUARY

CHAPTER 1 ... GENEALOGY CONNECTS

My Connection to the Tuesday Afternoon Club, 1895
Anthony Letter Addressees: *Mrs. Annie Pillsbury Young* and
The Tuesday P.M. Club, 1903

CHAPTER 2 ... WOMEN'S SUFFRAGE

My Connection to Susan B. Anthony
Letter: Susan B. Anthony, 1903

CHAPTER 3 ... A FATHER AND HIS SON

My Connection to William E. Greenleaf
Letter: William E. Greenleaf, 1960

CHAPTER 4 ... LOSS AND HOPE

My Connection to Arie E. Greenleaf
Letter: Arie E. Greenleaf, 1963

Chapter 1

Genealogy Connects

*My Connection to T.P.M., the Tuesday Afternoon Club
Susan B. Anthony addressed her 1903 letter to Mrs. Annie Pillsbury
Young and to The Tuesday P.M. Club in Manhattan, Kansas.*

SUSAN B. ANTHONY (1820–1906) is renowned in American history for her total dedication to women's suffrage, women's rights, and for the abolition of slavery. From her Quaker heritage, she embraced equality before God as a motivation for a lifetime devoted to the causes which would advance the needs of all people. She famously said, "Men, their rights, and nothing more; women, their rights, and nothing less."

When Anthony died March 13, 1906, at age eighty-six, women were still fourteen years away from obtaining the right to vote. Finally in 1920, the Nineteenth Amendment to the U.S. Constitution established women's suffrage and became known as the "Susan B. Anthony Amendment." The U.S. Treasury Department honored Anthony in 1979 by creating a one-dollar coin stamped with her image.

In January 1903 Anthony composed a personal letter to her good friend, Annie Pillsbury Young (1858–1942), and addressed it to Young and to *The Tuesday P.M. Club* in Manhattan, Kansas, the organization founded in 1895 by my Great-Grandmother, Mary Ursula Kessler Vandivert

(1841–1906). Her warm and poignant letter was timely, because Anthony died three years later, two months after Mary died from cancer.

My great-grandmother's devotion to faith and her commitment to the power of education for the community, especially for the betterment of women and the improvement of their lives, led to the club's formation, as revealed in numerous biographical remembrances. On January 18, 1906, two days after her death, an article appeared on page five of *The Manhattan Nationalist Supplement* which notes:

> [Vandivert] was a thorough bible student and during her life in Manhattan her talent for teaching has been of great service to her church and Y.M.C.A. [YWCA]. To this class of young women she devoted the last strength she had to give and counted it a joy to lead them to the rock of faith upon which her life was builded.

Mary was orphaned at a young age and raised by her grandparents, Samuel Alvord (1784–1872) and Ursula Smith Alvord (1793–1864), in Hamilton, Hancock County, Illinois, having moved there from New York following the death of her father, Philip Kessler (1819–1843). According to the *Genealogy of the Alvord Family*, Samuel's father Daniel Alvord *was a Massachusetts soldier in the Revolutionary War*. Daniel's service was honored in 1914 when Mary's daughter, my Grandmother Harriet Vandivert Remick (1874–1958), became a member of the DAR (*Daughters of the American Revolution*). I was fortunate to join in 1971 and am a member of the Abraham Kuykendall Chapter in Flat Rock, North Carolina.

The genealogy booklet also presents aspects of Samuel and Ursula's lives that speak to their characters, so representative of our country's early years. He was *a soldier in the War of 1812 and a pioneer Baptist preacher for over 60 years ... A pure life was his example. Sincerely devoted to his religion he lived for others. Heaven is his reward.* Ursula is described as *a daughter of Oliver Smith, a Revolutionary soldier from Connecticut ... a faithful wife, a devoted and affectionate mother.* The account continues, *[They] while each being a second companion to the other, had the rare experience of celebrating their 'Golden Wedding' November 20, 1863.*

Their daughter, Harriet Bowers Alvord Kessler (1822–1847), was Mary's mother, who remarried but tragically died soon after giving birth to a second daughter. The love and example Mary received from her grandparents led to a life committed to others. She became a teacher and moved to Bethany, Missouri, in 1871 with her uncle, an attorney, and taught in the local schools until she met and married Dr. Robert Henry Vandivert

(1819–1887) two years later, a widower with four sons. His children became hers, and all rejoiced together in the birth of both a daughter and sister a year later, my Grandmother Harriet.

She was born into a long line that reaches back into American history, with Robert Vandivert's ancestry connecting to the Dutch settlement of New Amsterdam, which served as the capital of the colony of New Netherland. The English took possession in 1664 and renamed the city New York for the Duke of York. Robert's grandfather, John, fought for independence from England as a corporal in the Revolutionary War, a tradition carried forward when Robert served in the Civil War. According to military documents, he was a surgeon in Burris's 6th Battalion, a State Militia Infantry from Bethany, and then was commissioned as *Surgeon of the Harrison County Regiment*, a battle unit in the Missouri Home Guard. He joined the Grand Army of the Republic (G.A.R.), the fraternal organization formed in 1866 to unite and honor war veterans from *the Union Army, the Union Navy, and the Marines*, an organization that lasted ninety years until the death of its last member. When Robert died March 29, 1887, his family received an official, handwritten condolence letter from the *T. D. Neal, Post No 124 Dept. of Mo. G.A.R.* A portion of the eloquently worded resolution expresses their high regard and is shared to acknowledge the faith and compassion that underpin our American heritage:

> Bethany, Mo. April 8, 1887
>
> Whereas our esteemed Comrade and fellow citizen Robert H. Vandivert has been called from his labors on this earth, to attend the "roll call" in the far beyond, therefore, be it, —
>
> Resolved ... By T. D. Neal, Post 124 G.A.R. that in his death, our Post has lost a true and worthy member, and the community a justly honored citizen, and his family a kind and loving husband and father.
>
> Resolved ... That our earnest sympathies are hereby tendered the bereaved family, and from Him who doeth all things well may they receive what comfort, in their sad bereavement which alone can heal their sorrows and assuage their pangs of grief.
>
> Resolved ... That as a mark of respect to our deceased Comrade, our Post rooms be draped in mourning for the next thirty days.

The serendipitous nature of life, in truth the reality of *My times are in Your hand* (Psalm 31:15 NKJV) is evident in their lives. When they married in 1873, Robert was fifty-four years old and had been widowed twice, and Mary was thirty-two and still single. I am blessed to descend from their union. The study of genealogy unveils an astonishing, even at times unbelievable story for every person, the happenings and "coincidences" that lead to the miracle of birth. Without their daughter, born in Robert's later years, no doubt a great joy to this father of four sons and a long hoped-for dream for Mary, neither the relationship nor the organization addressed in the Susan B. Anthony letter would have existed. This future historic connection finds additional support for its occurrence through Mary's character and compassion, as revealed in many writings, including the January 25, 1906, obituary in the *Bethany Republican-Clipper*, Bethany, Missouri:

> When [Mary Ursula Kessler] came into their father's home, but by a way all her own she at once became mother and companion to the boys, and Dr. A.H. [*Ashman Henry*] Vandivert] declares that she was all their own mother could have been to them and that her life was a continual inspiration to them for better things. He spoke also very touchingly of the careful nursing back to life a brother almost ready to pass away, saving his life.
> . . . [Mrs. Vandivert] was a woman of marked refinement and culture and wherever she went she always occupied a foremost position in every movement that meant better things for the community.
> . . . She is known and kindly remembered by many who bear testimony to her real worth as a sweet spirited christian (*sic*) woman who has made the world better by having lived in it.

Throughout her lifetime, Mary sought to improve not only living conditions (she established and worked with the Aid Society in the M.E. Church in Bethany), but she was also passionate about the benefits of learning. My Grandmother Harriet was only thirteen years old when her father unfortunately died, yet despite the deep loss, Mary was determined their daughter would advance and receive a college education, a rare occurrence for women in the late 1800s. This decision would ultimately lead to the founding of *The Tuesday P.M. Club*.

Chapter 2

Women's Suffrage

My Connection to Susan B. Anthony
Anthony's letter is a thoughtful reminiscence about family, friendship, and the *fight for freedom and the ballot* in the Civil War, as well as the hopes and efforts waged to secure women's *full suffrage* in Kansas.

MANHATTAN, KANSAS, APPROXIMATELY TWO hundred miles west of Bethany, Missouri, was home to the renowned Kansas State Agricultural College (KSAC), now Kansas State University. It was the first land-grant college to offer academic credits to women along with the degree program Domestic Economy. The department grew under the leadership of Professor Nellie Kedzie (Nellie Sawyer Kedzie Jones, 1858–1956), who taught at the college from 1882–1897. She introduced scientific research into the art of homemaking and became a national pioneer in the field of Home Economics. An article titled "One of the Oldest Meeting Groups is Tuesday Afternoon Club," written by T.P.M. member Lucile Berry Wolf for their Sixtieth Anniversary, was published in the 1955 Centennial Edition of *The Manhattan Mercury*. Wolf wrote, Harriet was enrolled as a student in Mrs. Nellie Kedzie's domestic science department at the college.

The story of Kedzie Jones's life is a fascinating track in American history when very few opportunities existed for women outside the home. Nellie grew up on a hard-working farm, which profoundly inspired the innovation she brought to her career. With the farm wife in mind, Nellie sought to improve domestic methodology, giving insight into better ways to accomplish household responsibilities. Details about her life reflect America's commitment to progress and opportunity.

Nellie graduated from KSAC in 1876 with a BS degree, taught at the college, and married Professor Robert Kedzie five years later. He became a Professor of Chemistry at (now) Mississippi State University but died from typhoid fever soon after they moved there. Nellie was asked to return to KSAC, initially as the Superintendent of Sewing. She earned her MS degree and became the faculty's first female full professor in 1887. Nellie is listed as Professor of Household Economy and Hygiene in the 1891 yearbook. She left KSAC in 1897 and became an Assistant Professor in the Department of Domestic Economy at brand-new Bradley Polytechnic Institute (now Bradley University, 1946) in Peoria, Illinois. The school was named for its founder, Lydia Moss Bradley (1816–1908), the institution established in memory of her deceased husband and six deceased children. Nellie was there until 1901, when she left and married Howard Jones. This was a fascinating discovery, because Bradley University is my alma mater.

... A Serendipitous Sidenote: While researching Nellie's Peoria years, I uncovered another thrilling fact, and it concerned my Grandfather Benjamin Luce Remick (1867–1947), who married Grandmother Harriet in 1904. A Cornell graduate, he became Professor and later Head of the Mathematics Department at KSAC, retiring professor emeritus after an extensive career. But my research found him listed, first, as a professor at Bradley Polytechnic Institute when Nellie was there. They were academic cohorts! Since his connection to Bradley had never been mentioned, I doubt my mother ever knew. The 1900 Peoria Census revealed that he and Nellie were also residents at the same boarding house for teachers on W. High Street! Dinnertime conversations undoubtedly included information about each person's life, so Nellie certainly shared stories about her years at KSAC. Her experiences must have resonated with my grandfather, and he was intrigued enough to pursue employment there. He and Harriet met in 1901 at a Military Reception on the KSAC campus, married, and had three children, Agnes, Benjamin Jr., and my mother Charlotte. Annie Pillsbury Young attended their wedding. The Lord has a plan. What may seem a coincidence is his hand upon our existence, the genetic and circumstantial workings of family history ever unfolding. *A man's mind plans his way [as he journeys through life], But the Lord directs his steps and establishes them* (Proverbs 16:9 AMP) . . .

After leaving Bradley, Nellie and her husband eventually moved to Smoky Hill Farm in Auburndale, Wisconsin, and she began writing a well-known column, "The Country Gentlewoman," published in *The Country Gentleman* magazine. She also had a radio program, was a nationwide lecturer, and was named the Home Economics Extension leader at the University of Wisconsin in 1918, retiring as professor emeritus in 1933.

Nellie received many other honors throughout her career. An 1898 campus landmark at KSAC was later named Kedzie Hall, and she received an honorary doctorate from KSAC in 1925. Her name is still recognized in our food industry. The "Aunt Nellie's" brand of beets and vegetables is still available commercially under her 1929 trademarked name, taken from the fictious character in her column known as Aunt Nellie who gave advice to a fictious niece, Janet. Throughout her career, Nellie demonstrated her passion and commitment to the betterment of life within the home through knowledge, a theme demonstrated in the lives of Mary Ursula Kessler Vandivert and Annie Pillsbury Young.

It was clear that Nellie's Household Economy program at KSAC offered the perfect opportunity for Grandmother Harriet. She moved to Manhattan in 1893 and found room and board with the Young family, where the idea for the T.P.M. Club was formed. Lucille Berry Wolf wrote in her 1955 article in *The Manhattan Mercury*:

> The young Miss Vandivert had been making her home with Mrs. Annie Pillsbury Young and Mrs. Vandivert, a widow, followed to take up residence here . . . The two older women became acquainted at once, becoming staunch friends, always engrossed in many fields of intellectual activity . . . The organization of the Tuesday Afternoon Club . . . came as the outgrowth of [their] rich and inspiring friendship . . . These two unusual women possessed far ranging, probing minds, each stimulating the other in broad intellectual quests, never restrained by lack of opportunity, domestic burdens or other circumstances. Mrs. Vandivert had an unsatiable interest in the study of law and in Missouri often lectured on legal matters. Young law students sat in her informal classes for the benefit of her instruction . . . Among the young matrons of Manhattan, the two friends found eager devotees of learning, training by parents in pioneer homes in habits of self education and self culture.

JANUARY

The Riley County Historical Society and Museum in Manhattan has a typed, hand-edited paper by Annie Pillsbury Young titled "Us As We Used To Be," a requested reminiscence for the Thirtieth Anniversary celebration of the T.P.M. Club in 1925. She mentions achievements through *the dynamic force of woman's organized effort*, including *prohibition and woman's suffrage*. Young describes the Club's beginning as the *tallow candle period* and paints a vivid picture of their fears and motives:

> [We] did not know which we feared most, the cynic smile of our husbands over our aspirations to be more intellectual, or the rather indulgent encouragement of the Domestic Science Club [D.S.C.], the one and only club then in town . . .
>
> Mrs. Vandivert, one of your founders, had the vision of "wonders to come" thru the power of Woman's Clubs but I thought only of our own betterment. While she dilated on the "Uplift idea" thru organized womanhood, I was digging away on the weekly programs and scouting around thru the town "high brows" for reference material for these were pre-library days. So she had the vision and I, as ever, lived one day at a time. [Annie's search for "reference material" led to her involvement in establishing the local library. She was also Manhattan's first female Postmaster after her father retired from the position.]

The mutual vision shared by Mary and Annie came to fruition on February 18, 1895, the founding date of T.P.M., the name later expanded to the *Tuesday Afternoon Club* (Wolf, 1955). Mary's utmost goal was *self-improvement*, and the Club Motto was taken from "Night Thoughts" by famous English poet Rev. Edward Young (1683–1765), chosen to express the ultimate value and intent of knowledge, *How empty learning and how vain is art, But as it mends the life and guides the heart*. Their meetings were held twice a month from mid-September through May, their programs designed *to support mental growth and interests of both cultural and entertainment value* (Wolf, 1955).

The first page of each *T.P.M.* annual program booklet states, *Founder, Mrs. Mary Ursula Vandivert, 1895*. Young was its first secretary. The first two women listed under *Past Presidents* are *Mary Ursula Vandivert, 1895–1897* and *Annie Pillsbury Young, 1897–1899*. Also listed as a past president is my grandmother, *Harriet Vandivert Remick, 1915–1916*. The list of *Associate Members* includes my mother, *Mrs. Charlotte Remick Brubaker*. In my possession are several *T.P.M.* booklets, mementos of a valued time in America.

Each contains the reflective poem written by Annie Pillsbury Young that is as true today as it was then:

> Most of life is to be endured
> Part of it overcome
> A bit of it ignored—
> Most of it thoroughly enjoyed
> And all of it
> Appreciated
> For therein lies the development of the soul.

The thrilling discovery of my Great-Grandmother Mary Vandivert's connection with Susan B. Anthony occurred when I came across The Dobkin Family Collection of Feminism, a tremendous resource for historical information concerning women's rights. Based in New York, their website states they have *original letters and manuscripts, annotated and inscribed books, personal diaries* which *chronicle women's advancements*. I'm deeply grateful to The Dobkin Family Collection for sharing Anthony's envelope and letter. Certainly, their mission dovetails with the story of Annie Pillsbury Young and Mary Kessler Vandivert, *women who envisioned and brought about real societal change* (https://www.dobkinfeminism.org/).

There are conclusions to this story. The Tuesday Afternoon Club remained an important, active Manhattan, Kansas, organization for 118 years until its final year, 2012–2013, its longevity a testimony to its founders. Also, my great-grandmother's life comes full circle with two articles published on January 18, 1906. *The Manhattan Nationalist Supplement* concludes its touching announcement concerning the passing of Mary Ursula Kessler Vandivert:

> In 1895 she organized the T.P.M. club with twelve charter members, six of whom acted as honorary pall bearers. She was its first president and also was a member of the D.S.C. She was a great sufferer during the past year and a half but bore all with such patience cheerfulness (*sic*) that her death came at last as a shock to her friends.

And *The Manhattan Republic* eloquently offers a profound statement concerning Mary's vision and reason for founding the T.P.M. Club. May her vision be ours:

> [Vandivert] was . . . a leader in the study of the world's literature. She also led the thoughts of the women who were her pupils to

higher ideals and a broader, sweeter charity for each other. She upheld the true club idea that women learn to value each other for the talents and good qualities possessed, rather than be criticized for those they lacked.

Letter Envelope ~ Susan B. Anthony

The Return Address:

NATIONAL AMERICAN
WOMAN SUFFRAGE ASSOCIATION
RETURN TO
SUSAN B. ANTHONY

HONORARY PRESIDENT
17 MADISON STREET
ROCHESTER, N.Y.

The Postmark:

ROCHESTER, N.Y.
JAN 13
12-PM
1903

The Address:

Mrs. Annie Pillsbury Young
For-Sec'y-The Tuesday P.M. Club
Manhattan
Kansas

Letter ~ Susan B. Anthony, 1903

National American Woman Suffrage Association
Member National Council of Women

Honorary Presidents {ELIZABETH CADY STANTON, 250 West 94th Street, New York
{SUSAN B. ANTHONY, 17 Madison Street, Rochester, N.Y.
President, CARRIE CHAPMAN CATT Recording Secretary, ALICE STONE BLACKWELL
208 American Tract Society Building, New York 3 Park Street, Boston, Mass.

Vice-President-at-Large, REV. ANNA H. SHAW Treasurer, HARRIET TAYLOR UPTON
4104 Powelton Avenue, Philadelphia, Pa. Warren, Ohio

Corresponding Secretary, KATE M. GORDON Auditors {LAURA CLAY, Lexington, Ky.
2008 American Tract Society Building, New York {MARY J. COGGESHALL
554 Seventh Street, Des Moines, Iowa
NATIONAL HEADQUARTERS, 2008 AMERICAN TRACT SOCIETY BUILDING, N.Y.
Office of the Honorary President, Rochester, N.Y.

Jan. 13, 1903

Annie Pillsbury Young,
My dear friend:

 I was very glad to hear from you, and know that you still lived though with an added name, which looks as though you were growing <u>Young</u> to say the least. I remember well the days we were at Manhattan, Mrs. Stanton and I, your uncle and aunt and you. I think your father was alive then, was he not ? and how after the meeting we went over to Judge Humphreys, and how kind all were to us. It was a hard campaign, but those old Free State settlers gave us the best they had. It seems a long time ago, and in another sense, but a short time.

 The last time I was at Manhattan I was with Mrs. Laura M. Johns I think, what was the man's name who gave me passes on the R.R. ? we were invited to his house to tea. Very nearly all are gone on to the beyond now, only a few of us left, like mile posts to mark the way. The incident of the Post office I do not remember,—but as we all grow older we see the relation of the <u>ballot</u>,—of those holding the right to it,—and <u>the offices</u> in the gift of the government. Women must learn that all they receive of official-plums is as a <u>privilege</u>:—When they vote, they will have something they can <u>pay</u> in exchange for the office. Oh, it seems as simple as the A—B—C— and yet the masses seem not to understand the principle on which <u>government</u> <u>favors</u> are <u>partitioned</u> out.

 Kansas has had two trials with woman suffrage amendments, voting a little over <u>one</u> <u>third</u> in favor. It is "three times and out." So if the present Legislature, when it gets through with electing its Senator vouchsafes to re-submit the question, I prophesy that <u>two</u> <u>thirds</u> of the men, not <u>one third</u>, will vote to give women the <u>full</u> suffrage. You have the school and municipal vote, which amount to but little without the State and National vote, so I hope for the day to come when <u>full</u> <u>suffrage</u> will be granted to the women of Kansas.

 Yes, I feel quite as much <u>State</u>-<u>pride</u> in Kansas as I do in New York, or Massachusetts and keep posted in all the doings through my brother's paper, <u>The</u> <u>Leavenworth</u> <u>Times</u>. I read it every morning. It is thirty-six hours after you are reading it, but I get the Kansas news. My other brother, J. Merritt of Fort Scott, who died so suddenly two years ago, was even more thoroughly a Kansan than is D.R. but he was a quiet man. He was in the John Brown battle of August 1856 at Osawatomie, went through all the border ruffian times, then was four years in the civil war from 1861 to 1865!! How the men did fight for <u>freedom and the ballot</u> for themselves, and yet having won the victory, how <u>very</u>, <u>very</u> slow they are in giving to women the boon for which their wives, mothers, sisters and daughters suffered as much as they. Who could have believed they would have voted down womans' (*sic*) equal rights with themselves twice over? Let us hope and pray that the generation of men who will vote upon the question the next time will be more noble, more just, than were those of the two preceding generations, for the two elections were twenty-seven years apart, so that the vast majority were new voters, either by birth or emigration.

With respect for the women of Kansas in general, and for the members of your Tuesday Afternoon Club in particular, I am,

> Affectionately yours,
> Susan B. Anthony

Chapter 3

A Father and His Son

My Connection to William E. Greenleaf
This 1960 letter is a compassionate sharing of a father's heart
for his son, revealing his own sensitive reflection on finding one's
purpose and aim in life.

THE PI BETA PHI sorority house, where I had recently been initiated, was on the corner across the street from the Bradley University campus in Peoria, Illinois. The top floor of the freshman dormitory, Burgess Hall, overlooked both Main Street and the sorority house beyond and provided a busy view from my dorm room window. As a newly active sorority member, it was easy to dash over when needed. On a lovely Friday evening, May 12, 1967, friends and I stopped by the house before making our way to a joint fraternity/sorority event at Bradley Park, with dinner planned at nearby Hunt's Drive-In. We popped in and saw our sorority sister, Amy, talking earnestly to a gentleman we had never seen before. He was cute, and in the group introductions our eyes met. With a twinkle of curiosity, we exchanged half-smiles, and in that brief encounter, the course of my life changed forever. After we left, he asked Amy for my name and phone number and was told he could only date one sorority sister at a time. He told her it had been nice knowing her, and, as the saying goes, "the rest is history."

JANUARY

The next day the phone rang on the only TWO rotary-dial telephones available on our entire dormitory floor, one at each end of a long hallway, and it was for me. I was in the third room from the wall phone and went to answer the call. It was him. Our conversation led to a date that night, which I initially refused. I had turned down other offers to study for a test, but he changed my mind. Wearing my pale pink dress, I entered the dormitory lobby filled with expectant young men, all other areas in the dorm off limits, and saw him waiting across the room, attired in his blue paisley sports jacket. After signing out for the evening, required in 1967, we got into his red Thunderbird and drove away. The date, however, almost ended a minute later when casual questions revealed I was only a freshman, and he was ten years older!

With a bit of an air, I made clear he could take me home if he didn't like it, but instead, we headed out into an evening filled with a variety of activities. We went to a movie but left after thirty minutes since our minds were on each other and not on the screen before us. We danced to "When I Fall in Love" at the Ramada Inn, and the coincidence seemed "a sign." Next was a stop at Kramer's (renamed Jumer's Castle Lodge in 1970), its Bavarian themed décor making it a favorite destination. Finally, we ended up at Monical's Pizza. After an evening when we both simply "knew," he proposed at midnight under the maple tree near the clock tower on the Bradley campus. As it struck twelve o'clock on a misty night, I said, "Yes," on this our first date.

The next day, I called my mom from that same wall telephone and said something like, "I went on a date last night with a guy I just met, and we got engaged. But I prayed about it!" She drove up the next weekend from our home in Webster Groves, Missouri, to meet him over a steak dinner at the Ramada Inn, where we had danced the week before. She encouraged us to wait until I finished school, but that didn't happen. Arie E. Greenleaf (1939–2004) and I were married three months later in August, a lovely wedding my parents kindly and generously provided. I was eighteen, a month shy of nineteen, and he had just turned twenty-eight. Certainly, making a quick decision like this is NOT recommended, but our marriage fortunately lasted, although not without the usual challenges that threaten a commitment.

Thanks to my dear parents, again, I was able to continue my education and in 1970 received a BS in Elementary Education. Our very adored son, Arie Todd, was born in 1972. Our journey to almost thirty-seven years of marriage included times of uncertainty and many moves. Thankfully, love for each other and a renewed and redemptive relationship with the Lord many years prior to my husband's cancer diagnosis and death in July 2004 allowed us to overcome the mistakes, sins, and struggles common in life.

Being a member of Arie's family has been a deep joy, his parents and siblings very dear to my heart. His mother and father, Mary Vanderhorst Greenleaf Campen (1921–2005) and William Eugene "Gene" Greenleaf (1915–1975) were wonderfully supportive and loving. They were part of the Greatest Generation (those born 1901–1927), with Gene serving in the U.S. Army Air Force in World War II and stationed in Colorado. He was a gentle, loving, humble man, devoted to the three most important relationships in life: faith, family and friends. He worked tirelessly for thirty-five years as an engineer in planning at Caterpillar Inc. before his untimely, heartbreaking death from an aneurism in 1975. His funeral service was held at Westminster Presbyterian Church in Peoria, with the Rev. Dr. William R. O'Neill officiating. The eulogy for my father-in-law honored his exemplary life, with the following excerpt an especially descriptive example of his sensitivity and kindness toward others:

> I gratefully acknowledge my indebtedness to Gene Greenleaf. He knew it is not easy to preach. How many times, before the Sunday service, Gene gripped my hand and said, "I am looking forward to your sermon this morning." I trust I can tell him sometime how much that meant to me! This is what I mean by saying that he lived affirmatively. That is no small matter in a time of negatives.

Could there be any greater tribute for an individual than to identify them as an encourager in this difficult world, someone who was affirming and uplifting? I think not. Gene's positivity blessed his family, as well. Arie was twenty years old and working toward a teaching degree at Illinois State Normal University (ISNU) in Normal, Illinois, about forty miles from Peoria, when he received an encouraging letter from his father. Mailed on January 19, 1960, Gene's letter is one of introspection, longing, and hope, an example of a father's love for his son.

. . . An Informative Sidenote: The Illinois State Legislature voted in 1963 to drop the word "Normal" from the school's original 1857 name, with the school officially becoming Illinois State University at Normal in 1964. When the word "Normal" was used in a school's name, it indicated they were a college or university that prepared individuals for a career in education, as the students were taught the "norms" or standards needed to become a teacher. The school changed its name once more in 1967, becoming Illinois State University (ISU), from which I graduated in 1989 with an MS degree in Education/Reading . . .

Letter ~ William E. Greenleaf, 1960

Dear Arie,

Just a few lines that you will know I haven't forsaken you. I trust you are getting on OK, and that each day and each week brings you closer to what your purpose and aim in life will be.

Although I must confess I am no authority on purpose and aim. For if I were to turn back the years of my life and start anew, I would I'm sure not falter <u>again</u> but make the purpose and aim of my life that of the ministry. And I would make it with a very strong impact. In fact I hope someday to be a better Christian even if my limitation is only that of a layman.

I'm sure that I understand your periods of wonder & indecision concerning your future for I very well remember my own exact feeling when I was your exact age.

And how I wish someone had opened their arms to me in consolation and given me the lift and the additional assurance which I needed at that time.

But <u>now</u> I do not want that someone to give me this extra lift. For now I have it, but the time is not yet at hand. But someday soon you shall see my decisive change.

I believe you would be a great asset to God in the ministry, Arie!

I must close for now. I shall pray hard for you.

We are having the O'Neill's over this Saturday evening. I wish you could be here.

I can pick up you, Carolyn [Arie's sister, 1940–2019], and the Shorts girl.

With Love,
Your Father

JANUARY

Letters are a fascinating revelation of yearning, hopes, dreams, and circumstances that are either directly expressed or understood. Their sensitive insights are usually applicable for the recipient, written as the future lies ahead with all its unknown twists and turns, but the author's heart is also revealed. Arie graduated in 1966 from ISU at Normal with a BS in Education. He was a "Home Counselor" at McKinley School in Peoria when we met and married, the school where I later did my student teaching. He decided on a counseling career and began his graduate studies in psychology at Bradley and received his MA degree in 1971. For over twenty years Arie worked off and on at counseling centers in various states, sometimes teaching part time, sometimes with his own private practice on the side, and sometimes his practice stood alone. Along the way, however, we also started several businesses, because Arie was forever the entrepreneur.

One of our most notable businesses was our first venture, The Greenleaf Shoppe, a gift store we operated from 1974–1977 in downtown Minocqua, a delightful tourist community in Northern Wisconsin. Many years later in 1992, we started Rapture Inc. where we made pewter jewelry on machines Arie built from junk yard parts. Initially we made Christian camp logos and attached them to necklaces and keyrings. From there we transitioned into jewelry for sororities and fraternities, then logos for colleges and universities, for Special Olympics, and for special events. We miraculously sold our business for $15,000 one month before Arie died, astonished and grateful for the couple who knew about our situation and appeared "out of the blue" and bought it! We had kept Rapture going through the year of Arie's cancer treatments, the requisite chemotherapy, surgery, and radiation, but were too overwhelmed to attempt a sale. Truly, though not surprisingly, the Lord stepped in. Rapture Inc. had been our sole support for twelve incredible years that included four moves, and I always tell people, "You know there is a God who loves you, because our initial pieces were not very attractive, and our business should never have survived." But it did, praise God, for he led us all the way.

When Arie's father wrote his letter in 1960, he could never have imagined how life would unfold for his son. He hoped he would go into the ministry, but life intervened and that dream was scuttled. Until Dad's death in 1975, his prayers undergirded Arie and his family and were a tremendous foundation we simply didn't understand or appreciate. Children and grandchildren will never comprehend the blessings received from the depth and volume of prayers lifted for them by their parents and grandparents. Arie and I certainly didn't, at least not until we were much older and understood the truth to *pray without ceasing* (1 Thessalonians 5:17 NKJV) for our family. Patrick and I married two years after Arie died, and we continue to faithfully call upon the Lord every day, all day, knowing this truth from Lamentation 3:22–24 NKJV:

> *Through the Lord's mercies we are not consumed,*
> *Because His compassions fail not.*
> *23 They are new every morning;*
> *Great is Your faithfulness.*
> *24 "The Lord is my portion," says my soul,*
> *"Therefore I hope in Him!"*

Chapter 4

Loss and Hope

My Connection to Arie E. Greenleaf
This 1963 letter reveals a young man seeking to *understand the reasoning behind* the death of his beloved wife.

WHEN I MET ARIE in 1967, he shared the tragic loss of his first wife, Sandra "Sandy" Jean Green (1942–1962), from Rockford, Illinois. They were students together at Illinois State Normal University, and a black and white photo from the *I.S.N.U. Sweetheart Ball 1961* reveals the joy they found in each other. Sandra is lovely in a white, off-the-shoulder satin dress, short white gloves, and a wrist corsage. Arie is proud, handsome, and smiling by her side. That same year, she was diagnosed with cancer.

After receiving this devastating news, Arie immediately asked her to marry him, wanting to give Sandy the wedding she always desired. A very telling and sensitive letter by her mother, Ruth Green, was written to Arie's parents in July 1961 confirming her lifelong dream:

> The wedding is going to be a little on the big side I'm afraid, but Sandra has talked about "her wedding" since she was about six years old—so we will try and give her a nice wedding . . . Arie has certainly been wonderful, and a great help during Sandra's illness and we hope that they will continue to be just as happy with whatever

time God decides they are to have ... We are slightly confused with
all that is happening this summer, but we keep trying.

Prayers for healing accompanied all the planning for the September 8, 1962, wedding. Photographs from that day show a very happy couple, with parents, siblings, and friends celebrating the joyous occasion. But underneath the smiles and good wishes, cancer continued its course. Sandra died three months later, on December 19, 1962.

When Arie talked about her death and that period of his life, he always described himself as leaving the cemetery bitter at God and not wanting anything to do with Him since He didn't heal Sandy. She was a beautiful, kind, and loving woman, and what happened made no sense to him, nor would it to any of us. With every prayer, they believed she would be healed. When that didn't happen, his faith went into a tailspin to the point of rejecting God. Later, Arie understood that Sandy received eternal healing in the arms of her Savior, Jesus Christ, but her death at such a young age was difficult to accept. She was no longer with him and the family who loved her, and his resentment toward God festered and remained deep. Any thoughts about going into the ministry, as his father had hoped, were laid aside.

That fall Arie received a provisional teaching certificate and chose to stay in Rockford for several years, where he taught combined classes in grades three through twelve at a small country school. Those were increasingly lonely years, but he loved his job and always pointed out his school on our many trips from Central Illinois to Northern Wisconsin. As we sped by on Highway 39, the school that was a solace in his grief stood in the distance, a reminder of both his joy and his sorrow.

In my book *Hand of Mercy, A Story of God's Grace* (AE Books, 2015), Arie's experience and what happened eighteen years later is shared. Completely broken and in despair, even suicidal, he turned to the Lord and prayed, "Oh, God, I don't know if you're there or not, but I've made a mess of my life! If you want it, you can have it." He kept this tremendous turning point a secret, and it was a year before he told me. Arie needed emotional and spiritual healing, which requires time, for God heals from the inside out. However, his silence is also a reflection on the state of our tenuous marriage and my own errant heart. God had much work to do in me, as well, and thankfully he did it.

After my mother-in-law died, I received a thick packet of letters Arie had written to his parents. Busy at the time, I hastily tucked them away in a storage box. Now, years later, thinking perhaps there might be a letter that would lend itself to this book, I was surprised to find a typed letter Arie mailed from Rockford on January 8, 1963, barely two weeks after Sandy's death.

Letter ~ Arie E. Greenleaf, 1963

Dear Mom and Dad,

Most everything is back to normal except for my missing Sandy. Life is kind of blank without her. But all else is pretty wonderful; Mr. and Mrs. Green have taken me in as a real son and Judy [Sandy's sister] tries to be half way nice every once in a while. My kids are still the same bunch of tremendous live-wires. I've been working the tar out of both them and myself. Why they don't even have time to blow their noses during school and at recess, and I don't think they even bother to notice.

I've been writing a few letters believe it or not. I thought I had better before I am forgotten by even the few people I know.

My visiting was very trying as I found my situation changed so much from theirs. I wanted so much to have what they were having, but I guess the Lord is taking me in another direction. It's strange what He does; I simply do not understand the reasoning behind it, I guess. But He has been pretty wonderful to me, He has shown me a great deal of truth, more and more I feel His power working in and through me. What a wonderful feeling! It's going to be the best year of my life I think. I have been made aware of the key to making every day the best day one can live.

*"First, rise each morning with the truth that God is surely directing our lives and working out His truth through us; therefore what we do is of great importance. No matter what happens He will be with us and give us the strength to be the captain of the situation."

*"Second, live in God's grace. Never start or end any day with a guilt feeling. Each night talk over with God all the things that have been done the good and the bad. And then, give the whole day to God, both the good and the bad. He'll take both and set us free from our guilt so that it will not get in between us and other people and our responsibilities. Then we can look all life in the face confident that we with God can tackle any situation."

JANUARY

*"Third, live beyond ourselves. No man is truly happy for very long when he looks out for only "number one." The fulfillment of the Law lies in accepting other people's problems as our very own. Only when we are living for others can we do God's will and be happy." There they are one, two, and three. The hard yet most rewarding rules to fruitful living.

I'm sorry I didn't make it home but perhaps it was best I wasn't feeling too well. I'll see you sometime in the near future though.

Give my love to the family. Tell them to behave themselves. I'll write again soon,

Love, your son,

Arie

. . . An Explanatory Sidenote: The resource for the quoted material is unknown. Arie typed all of it in one paragraph and penciled in the quotation marks before and after each point. I made paragraphs of the First, Second, and Third listing for better clarity. Each ordinal number was underlined in pencil . . .

This astonishing letter was a puzzlement, considering what Arie always told me about his attitude toward God when Sandy died. While it was wonderful to discover his faith was meaningful and comforting in the weeks immediately following her death, everything he had ever said about that time made the letter very surprising. I'm sure Arie would agree. Pondering this discrepancy, I understood when loss is deep, sometimes our faith falters, and our resentment becomes a cold rebellion. Certainly, when I met him in 1967, Arie was far from God and intended to stay there. Apparently, "leaving the cemetery shaking his fist at God and wanting nothing to do with Him" occurred later, a result of his increasing pain and loneliness. Thankfully, his anguish eventually brought him to his knees, and God healed the deep hurt and anger.

Through the years, Arie described his faith at the time of Sandy's death as "an intellectual game and a college sport." He had taken pleasure debating the issues of religion, but the debate excluded a personal, heart relationship with Jesus. He felt the well-known saying, "People miss heaven by eighteen inches, the distance between the head and the heart"[1] applied to him. Perhaps that relationship was missing when Sandy died, although his letter speaks to a sincerity in his belief and relationship that is hard to deny. Maybe in his eagerness to "do something," he relied on his own effort to handle the grief and missed the command to simply abide in the Lord.[2]

Relying on our own personal effort and strength to handle sorrow, let alone the smallest details of daily life, will lead to frustration, anger, and despair. Sometimes grief takes control, and we lose sight of God.

In the end, the Lord is merciful and knows the truth of our hearts.[3] He was always waiting for Arie to turn to him, as he waits for all of us, and when that happened God answered his desperate plea. With complete assurance,[4] Arie gave his heart and soul to Jesus Christ, *the author and finisher of our faith*,[5] and is now in heaven with the Lord, and that is a glorious "Hallelujah!" I can only imagine the joy his earthly father, Gene, felt *when he ran to his son*[6] to welcome Arie Home.

[1] *Therefore, since a promise remains of entering His rest, let us fear lest any of you seem to have come short of it.* [2] *For indeed the gospel was preached to us as well as to them; but the word which they heard did not profit them, not being mixed with faith in those who heard it.* [3] *For we who have believed do enter that rest* (Hebrews 4:1–3a NKJV).

[2] *Abide in Me, and I in you. As the branch cannot bear fruit of itself, unless it abides in the vine, neither can you, unless you abide in Me* (John 15:4 NKJV).

[3] *But the Lord said to Samuel, "Do not consider his appearance or his height, for I have rejected him. The Lord does not look at the things people look at. People look at the outward appearance, but the Lord looks at the heart"* (1 Samuel 16:7 NIV).

[4] *These things I have written to you who believe in the name of the Son of God, that you may know that you have eternal life, and that you may continue to believe in the name of the Son of God* (1 John 5:13 NKJV).

[5] *Looking unto Jesus, the author and finisher of our faith, who for the joy that was set before Him endured the cross, despising the shame, and has sat down at the right hand of the throne of God* (Hebrews 12:2 NKJV).

[6] *"So he got up and went to his father. But while he was still a long way off, his father saw him and was filled with compassion for him; he ran to his son, threw his arms around him and kissed him . . . 'for this my son was dead and is alive again; he was lost and is found'"* (Luke 15:20,24 NKJV).

FEBRUARY

CHAPTER 5 ... TEENAGE INSPIRATION

My Connection to Catherine Marshall
Letter: Ann Brubaker, 1964

CHAPTER 6 ... A GRACIOUS REPLY

My Connection to a Letter from Catherine Marshall
Letter: Catherine Marshall, 1964

Chapter 5

Teenage Inspiration

My Connection to Catherine Marshall
This 1964 letter is my 15-year-old, tenth-grade expression of gratitude
for the inspirational book which *influenced my life greatly.*

CATHERINE (WOOD) MARSHALL (1914–1983) wrote *A Man Called Peter, The Story of Peter Marshall* (1951), a compelling account about her Scottish immigrant husband who became both Senior Pastor at New York Avenue Presbyterian Church in Washington, DC, and Chaplain of the U.S. Senate. Her book captured my imagination and my heart with an affirmation of the faith I'd known since childhood.

The Rev. Dr. Peter Marshall (1902–1949) was born in Coatbridge, N. Lanarkshire, Scotland. He grew up determined to serve in the Royal Navy and attempted to join before he was fifteen years old, but God, or "the Chief" (Marshall, *A Man Called Peter*, 3), as Peter called him, had different plans. As this door and others closed, another opened, and Peter was "tapped on the shoulder" for ministry (Marshall, *A Man Called Peter*, 3). He eventually found himself on a passage to America to attend seminary, arriving at Ellis Island in April 1927.

The generosity of family and friends gave evidence of the Lord's hand upon Marshall's life, but he worked hard in jobs from Elizabeth, New Jersey, to Birmingham, Alabama, and onto his graduation in 1931 from Columbia

Theological Seminary in Decatur, Georgia. Each step along the way opened a remarkable future. While serving as the senior pastor at Westminster Presbyterian Church in Atlanta, Georgia, he met Catherine Wood, who was attending Agnes Scott College. They were married in 1936. The following year Marshall accepted a ministerial call to the church where President Abraham Lincoln had worshipped in the 1860s, New York Avenue Presbyterian. Every Sunday Peter's riveting sermons, preached with his Scottish brogue, captivated the overflowing congregation. So many people came to hear him, loudspeakers were implemented to project the message to the many attendees standing outside, even on rainy days.

Meaningful friendships formed between Marshall and the prominent Senators and Congressmen in his congregation. Their admiration led to the January 1947 election of Peter Marshall to serve as the fifty-seventh Chaplain of the U. S. Senate. His prayer at the opening of each daily session was short, insightful, and relevant, so much so, he became known as "the conscience of the Senate" (Marshall, *A Man Called Peter*, 222).

Peter developed heart disease and tragically died on Tuesday, January 25, 1949, at 8:15 a.m. (Marshall, *A Man Called Peter*, 235–238). He was only forty-six years old. His death was a devastating loss to everyone who knew him, but God would continue to grow Marshall's impactful ministry through the many subsequent books written by his wife, Catherine Marshall. God's love for us, his mercy and grace, and the daily and eternal hope we have through faith in his Son, Jesus Christ, are realities still presented today through the recorded words and story of the Rev. Dr. Peter Marshall. His ministry and Catherine's writings have had a profound and unique influence on America, and on me.

From second grade through my freshman year of college, I lived on Fairview Avenue, three doors down from the First United Methodist Church in the St. Louis, Missouri, suburb of Webster Groves. Since we were members and lived practically "next door" to the church, it was an easy walk up the street to regularly attend Sunday School and the worship services, the choir practices, and the MYF (Methodist Youth Fellowship). On "Methodist Student Day," June 6, 1965, James Brown and I preached a sermon to the congregation titled "Lost Beat." Fortunately, I still agree with my conclusion:

> I firmly believe in borrowed advice—I firmly believe in asking God to help me with my relationship to my parents, family, friends—to help me in my search for finding myself—to help me

find my purpose in life. In short, I . . . well, not just me but each one of us participating in this service, and those who aren't . . . we believe in God's promise for help. Lost beat . . . lost understanding . . . lost generation? I should say not—not with God's help.

Being involved in church activities meant everything in my formative years, but the property and building itself provided hours of fun. Summer softball games in the parking lot were epic and dovetailed nicely with practicing my tennis skills against the church wall. Roller skating in the lot and up and down the street consumed much of the rest of my summer vacation.

One of my best friends, Virginia "Ginny" Burch, lived next door to the church. When Arie and I were married on a beautiful Saturday afternoon with my wonderful pastor the Rev. John Ward officiating, she was one of my bridesmaids, along with another dear childhood friend, Jan Schnieders. I was one of Ginny's bridesmaids when she and Smith Reed were married several years later.

Ginny and I spent countless hours playing on the steps of the multi-level church entrance fronting North Bompart Avenue, a unique stage upon which an untold number of cherished memories were made. We twirled batons on the landing, entertaining ourselves and the cars that drove by, sometimes with a honk and a wave. Often an older couple out for an evening stroll stopped to chat. We played secretary, each wearing rimmed glasses without the glass, the left palms of our hands a notebook upon which we "took dictation." Sometimes we were families living side by side, the middle railing dividing our "houses." Until we were old enough to become Candy Stripers at Barnes Hospital in downtown St. Louis, where we both received the coveted, pink-striped cap representing over 100 hours of dedicated service, we were the nurses we hoped to become. My cap is still in my scrapbook, but Ginny was the one to fulfill that dream. The scenarios we acted out were as limitless as our imaginations. These delightful childhood reflections are lustrous memories that bring immense gratitude.

Along with the joy experienced at church, reading has always been a favorite pastime. I attempted to read and own every Nancy Drew Mystery book available back then, immediately spending my weekly one-dollar allowance on the next book in the series. I built my library on the literary foundation that began in third grade at Avery School when I was introduced to *The Boxcar Children* by Gertrude Chandler Warner (1890–1979). This adventurous and enchanting story caught my fancy, and its expanded series is still popular.

However, it was the numerous biographies that lined our classroom bookshelves that were the most thought provoking. They belonged to the series called *Childhood of Famous Americans*, published by Bobbs-Merrill of Indianapolis, Indiana, beginning in 1932. Reading about Florence Nightingale and Clara Barton, about Davy Crockett and Daniel Boone, or about Betsy Ross and Benjamin Franklin and the challenges and accomplishments that made them famous was enormously inspiring. The original books were a solid orange in color with a plain black title, the later editions branching out in design. Illustrations were in black silhouette, a perfect accompaniment highlighting the endeavors that fascinated. I devoured every book and looked for more.

. . . A Genealogical Sidenote: It was astounding and humbling to discover that the remarkable Benjamin Franklin (1706–1790) and I descend from sisters Abiah and Joanna, daughters of Peter Folger (1617–1690) and Mary Morrell (1620–1704) from Nantucket, Massachusetts, making us first cousins eight times removed. I could never have imagined . . .

Intrigued by biographies in grade school, it was natural to read about Peter Marshall in high school. The movie *A Man Called Peter*, based on the book, premiered in 1955 starring Richard Todd as Peter Marshall and Joan Peters as Catherine Wood. It came out on television years later, and since I loved the book, I was eager to see it. In awe of Peter's life and message, I wrote a heartfelt letter to Catherine Marshall, wanting to share the impact of their story. The original draft of my 1964 letter, penciled on lined school paper and edited with mark-outs, circles, and arrows, has survived all these years and remains a sincere expression of my youthful heart.

Letter ~ Ann Brubaker, 1964

Dear Mrs. Marshall,

    I feel at a loss for words on what I want to tell you, but the best way is directly, so that's how I'll be. Your book *A Man Called Peter* has influenced my life so greatly that I felt it was necessary to share it with you. That's why you're reading a letter from a fifteen-year-old girl, completely inexperienced in this type of "confession," for that's somewhat how it is. I'm confessing my deep admiration for Mr. Peter Marshall and his wonderful sermons, and for you and the tremendous book you wrote.

    I read it and loved it. Mr. Marshall's life was so full of meaning and closeness to God that I knew that God had to be. Please don't misunderstand me, I have always believed in God, but this book opened up a new door. A light shone in showing me that God <u>really</u> cares for us, that if we honestly believe in Him and His powers of love and goodness for us, then nothing is impossible.

    In your book you quoted from Matthew 6:33 (KJV), "But seek ye first the kingdom of God, and his righteousness; and all these things shall be added unto you." Peter Marshall's life was a true representation of this passage. This passage and his life are what helped to change mine.

    Then I read Mr. Marshall's sermons, and ironically enough, the sermon "Sin in the Present Tense" seemed to have been written straight to me. My best friend was facing a problem that frightened us both. When I got home from her house I read that sermon, for no other reason than I hadn't finished the sermons, and I had wanted to before Sunday. <u>Everything</u> we had talked about was in that sermon. I couldn't help but believe what Mr. Marshall wrote, it was all so true. This is just a minor example, but yet important in my faith.

I hope I have explained to you, or at least shown you, the part your book has played in my life. It now has a truer meaning, and all because I got to know Peter Marshall and God through a wonderful book.

    I sincerely want to thank you for everything,
    Ann Brubaker

Chapter 6

A Gracious Reply

My Connection to a Letter from Catherine Marshall
This 1964 letter is a gracious expression of Catherine Marshall's
thankfulness that her book *A Man Called Peter* had created
a *personal bond and friendship* between us.
It was the thrill of a lifetime to receive her letter and a blessing to share.

SEVERAL MONTHS AFTER THE Rev. Dr. Peter Marshall died in early 1949, Catherine called upon the help of those who knew Peter well to read and choose twelve of his uplifting sermons to prepare for a book. She understood the public's longing for the continuation of her husband's ministry, and the Fleming R. Revell Company agreed to publish *Mr. Jones, Meet the Master* (1949). This ground-breaking, visionary work presents Peter Marshall's elegantly worded and strongly powerful sermons explaining the life-changing, gospel message of Jesus Christ. Peter prepared his sermons using a poetic structure to guide his presentation, and this discovery was maintained in the book and became a publishing first, making his sermons easy to read. *Mr. Jones, Meet the Master* was a resounding success.

Catherine went on to write two more books, *A Man Called Peter* (1951) and *To Live Again* (1957) before marrying Leonard LeSourd (1919–1996), executive editor of *Guideposts* magazine, in 1959. They shared a life of ministry that included a partnership with John and Elizabeth Sherrill to create a well-known Christian publishing company, Chosen Books, now affiliated with Baker Publishing Group. My personal library contains fifteen books by Catherine Marshall, each one read and cherished. Her writings personally reveal the Lord's mercy and demonstrate how to apply biblical principles and truth to the challenges, joys, and sorrows we all face. Catherine's honesty about her own struggles and how God worked in her life through them makes her inspired writings relatable and hopeful. The following books, listed in order of publication, have been especially important in shaping my understanding and application of faith: *Mr. Jones, Meet The Master* (1949); *A Man Called Peter* (1951); *To Live Again* (1957); *Beyond Ourselves* (1961); *John Doe, Disciple* (1963); the novel *Christy* (1967); *Something More* (1974); *Adventures in Prayer* (1975); *Meeting God at Every Turn* (1980); and the novel *Julie* (1984).

Catherine was a New York Times best-selling author, and her writing is forever timeless and relevant. Her books are available through Amazon.com or through Evergreen Farm Publishing, "The Home of the Works of Catherine Marshall." www.evergreenfarmpublishing.com

Letter ~ Catherine Marshall, 1964

February 4, 1964

Dear Miss Brubaker:

Through the years I have come to feel that gratitude is one of the greatest of all human qualities.

So few of us manage the follow-through to express gratitude, even when we feel like it. That is why a letter like yours, means so much to me. You did express appreciation—and so beautifully.

It also means more than you can possibly realize for me to know that you feel a personal bond and friendship with me through A MAN CALLED PETER.

Nothing ever pleased Peter Marshall so much as knowing that he had revealed God, His greatness, His love and caring, to teen-agers.

By the way, do you know about the latest book, JOHN DOE, DISCIPLE? It is a collection of Dr. Marshall's best sermons to young people, and Peter John wrote the Introduction. I think that you—and your friend too—would love it.

I know that the future holds great things for you, Ann, because your feet are set on the right path now, with the right Guide.

Everything good to you!
Cordially,
Catherine Marshall

MARCH

CHAPTER 7 . . . A MOTHER'S HEART

My Connection to Mary Vanderhorst Greenleaf
Letter: Mary Vanderhorst Greenleaf, 1960
Memoir: "Mary had a Baby!" 1976

CHAPTER 8 . . . EVER FORWARD

My Connection to Mary Vanderhorst Greenleaf Campen
Letter: Mary Vanderhorst Greenleaf, 1976
Poem: "Clara Carolyn" —Ann Brubaker Greenleaf Wirtz, 2019

Chapter 7

A Mother's Heart

My Connection to Mary Vanderhorst Greenleaf
This 1960 letter is a newsy, relatable sharing of a mother's love and
thoughtful observations on life, family, and the season when
the birds are getting to talk in spring-like tones.

MARY VANDERHORST GREENLEAF CAMPEN (1921–2005), my dear mother-in-law, was a creative, lovely woman who enjoyed classical music, reading, sewing, working in her flower garden, and cooking delicious meals. Daughter of a Presbyterian minister, second of nine children, Mary and her first husband, William Eugene "Gene" Greenleaf, married in 1938 and raised a wonderful family of five. Arie is the oldest. His siblings are mentioned in her letter, and their names and ages in 1960 are Carol, nineteen; Bill, seventeen; Margie (Mary Margaret), fourteen; Danny, seven.

When Mary died eight months after Arie's passing, I spoke at her service, sharing the vast impact she had made on our lives, including her love and appreciation for nature:

> Her love for flowers, especially the beautiful roses she grew, is legendary. I'll always remember her gardens, the spring columbine and peonies, the orange poppies nodding across the yard, her pots of pansies. What a treasured legacy she has given us. Of course, in thinking of her flowers, we must remember her birds, for the two

went together. I learned the names and varieties from her kitchen window. In reflecting on her children, is there a home without a garden or feeder? Not to my knowledge.

A sensitive, private person, Mary found fulfillment in creating a warm and inviting home. She cherished the simple beauty around her, an extension of her deep faith, which was also lived out in her desire to do what she could to help others. This heartfelt letter, which only a caring mother could write, was written to Arie when he was twenty and attending college at ISNU.

Letter ~ Mary Vanderhorst Greenleaf, 1960

March 21, 1960

Dear Arie,

    We enjoyed your visit at home so much. All of us liked Linda [Arie's date] very much. I'm glad everyone seemed to be happy about it.

    I'm sure Spring can't be far away. The almanac says a big snow storm again this weekend. Maybe it will be wrong. Anway the birds are getting to talk in spring-like tones. Saturday I was in the back yard and noticed some tulips up three or four inches. So nature seems to be impatient to start another season.

    Margie wasn't very sick with the measles. She was up most of the time after Monday. I won't be surprised if Danny has them about next weekend. It takes 2 to 3 weeks.

    I'm anxious to start house cleaning but think it's not very profitable as long as we have a fire in the furnace.

    The pictures turned out pretty good. I sent the first ones to Mother [Amy Kamberg Vanderhorst, 1897–1983]. I've had some others made which will be ready today. When I get them I'll let you have a set if you want them.

    I noticed that your letter was written better than usual. Fewer mistakes. Maybe it would be good practice to write letters often. Carol wrote a couple of times last week. She enjoyed her weekend at home, too.

    Sometimes I think we are pretty awful. Myself included. Lack of insight, maturity. And just when things get to going well suddenly they don't. All in all, I guess we're no better or worse than any other people.

    From time to time I've asked Danny about his S. School. What he studies, etc. Last night I was telling him I heard his group singing "Let My People Go" at Sunday School. So he wanted to know what it meant. I proceeded to tell him the story of Moses. He was so excited. Every once in a while he knew what came next. When I was <u>about</u> through he excused himself . . . Instead of coming back, he went to the piano and played some of his music. Nature must protect little minds. Here he was so intent on one thing. In a few minutes he was completely intent on another.

Bill finished his term paper yesterday. I read it and counted words for him. It was supposed to be 800–1200 words. I counted about 850. He writes very factual with absolutely no detail or colour. ["It was still good enough to receive an *A*," Bill explained with a smile, many years later.]

Here's hoping you are doing well! Study hard and take good care of yourself.

Love,
Mother

It's a joy reading my mother-in-law's letters. With a minimum of words, Mary touches on everyday events and emotions, conveying a compassionate sensitivity. On stationery outlined with pale blue forget-me-nots, Mother penned reflections on her first year of marriage to Gene and the birth of their first child, born in 1939, thirteen months after their June wedding. Father and son have matching middle names, but their baby was named for his grandfather, Arie Vanderhorst, a Dutch family tradition which has continued with our son Arie Todd and grandson Arie Aarush. Her inspiring reminiscence is a fascinating peek into rural, midwestern life in 1938 and 1939, revealing the simplicity and complexity of her world. Mary's underlying encouragement to embrace life with a tenacious and joyful spirit is delightfully shown through a portion of her 1976 memoir.

Memoir ~ Mary Vanderhorst Greenleaf, 1976

MARY HAD A BABY!

Mary had a baby! The baby's father was Gene. She was only seventeen years old when she conceived and eighteen years old when their baby was born . . .

Every precaution was taken to have the finest healthiest child. Mary wanted to get to bed on time so as not to disturb the baby's rest. In fact there was great deliberation as to whether a late movie would be advisable.

Their first year of marriage was to be the simplest, happiest, full of love and exploration of one another. There were a few minor upsets—no plumbing—no electricity—no heat except for an old stove in the kitchen. The cooking stove caught fire one day. Gene, using his adrenaline, carried the stove out the door. A task that would be great for two men under ordinary circumstances. It was a gasoline pressure range that could be dangerous . . .

Poverty was indeed their companion. Among the dwindling flock of hens was Bloomers. The pet rooster with legs so full, he looked like he was wearing bloomers. One day it was no meat or Bloomers. So Gene wrung his neck and Mary cooked him. But Alas! Neither could eat him.

The big treat of the week was on Saturday night, when they did their weekly shopping. An ice cream cone or a candy bar depending on the season.

Finally July came. All was in readiness. The basket lined. Every little garment hand stitched. A little blue quilt. Besides all these, friends bestowed their gifts so the expected one was well supplied, indeed!

Early one morning, Mary knew the baby was coming . . . It was a long hard birth and Mary would have just as soon been some place else.

But it was worth it all to receive such a beautiful, perfect little son. So tiny one could fit him in two hands.

With great pride he was introduced to family and friends. Attending church at less than two weeks old. So full of pride and wanting to share their precious son . . .

The incidents of Arie's early life were to ones of adventure, mixed liberally with sweetness, and a love of goodness. Indeed, after being hit by a car, school and play accidents it seemed a wonder that he survived.

After one spill falling off the back of a moving car, his mother Mary thought to herself, "One day I may lose my son. But if I do, he will have given me so much that I could never really lose. I have already received that gift of love and being loved which no one can take away."

Mary did lose her son with Arie's death to cancer in July, the day after he turned sixty-five. She died the following March. As with all parent and child relationships, they had their ups and downs, the usual issues that spring from a mother's desire for the best for her children. But they had a genuine love and caring for each other, so clear in their correspondence and evident when they were together. She was a mother through and through, and he was a son finding his own way, as it should be.

Chapter 8

Ever Forward

My Connection to Mary Vanderhorst Greenleaf Campen
This 1976 letter conveys the challenges of widowhood, when loneliness combines with ongoing house repairs and yard maintenance, and one feels *completely ignorant or haven't the strength to do them.*

THE LETTERS AND WRITINGS chosen for this book are reflections of our common humanity as experienced within our American story. Some have been more emotional than expected, their poignancy bringing tears of remembrance and gratitude. The following is an excerpt from a letter received one year after Gene's sudden and devastating death from an aneurism in 1975. Mary expresses the hard challenges often experienced after the loss of a beloved spouse.

Her revealing letter also mentions a trip to visit her oldest daughter and the comfort she received. Carol understood, for she had been widowed almost seven years earlier when her first husband, George Fell (1941–1969), died in a small airplane accident while moose hunting in Alaska, where they lived and taught school. Carol was six months pregnant with their first child. Arie flew to Wasilla to bring his sister home for the funeral held in George's hometown of Lexington, Illinois. Carol stayed with her parents in Peoria until their son, John, was born several months later. She went back to Alaska, eventually married her dear second husband, Butch Potterville, and they retired to South Dakota and Arizona in 2004. This loving sister-in-law died very suddenly in 2019. My poem conveys a bit of Carol's uniqueness:

> Clara Carolyn (1940–2019)
> Her given names are a
> nostalgic alliteration of sound
> clarifying who she was:
> *Clara*, Latin for
> "Clear, bright and famous,"
> *Carolyn* in Italian meaning "strong,"
> she possessed a spirit, kind and gracious.
>
> Her days were
> a concert of creativity
> filled with projects galore,
> from her extraordinary quilts
> treasured around the world,
> to the piano she cherished,
> her music lovingly unfurled.
>
> Carol, as she was known,
> lived life above the ordinary,
> embracing beauty in her home décor,
> her flowers, her sewing, her paintings,
> her hobbies astound,
> her doll collection especially dear,
> her culinary skills worthy of great renown.
>
> Her passing leaves an unfillable void,
> her earthly brightness has dimmed,
> yet sorrow finds peace
> in the Lord above
> and the family who awaited her there,
> health now restored and faith complete,
> Carol's life is a joy to share.

Letter - Mary Vanderhorst Greenleaf Campen, 1976

August 16, 1976

Dear Arie and Ann,

It was good of you to call yesterday. I'm sorry I wasn't more exuberant. Sometimes I feel sort of defeated and yesterday was one of those days. I've learned to do a great many things this past year but there are still a good many areas that I'm completely ignorant or haven't the strength to do them.

The neighbors watched the place while I was gone but also butchered my trees. I could sue them but then I wouldn't have anyone to watch my place. So I've got to get someone to repair the damage and seal the trees. Guess I could try to saw the limbs. The brake line on my bicycle needs something done to it. Guess I'll climb on the house and finish cleaning the gutters. Then I'll build up my muscles and move the lumber. Fix the leaky shower—find the rusty pipe in the basement.

I wished I could have stayed longer with Carol. She needed me and I wasn't lonesome. She also was able to help me with my inner thoughts as she had so much empathy for me. She understands my restlessness—loneliness—etc. They're talking about me spending Christmas with them or at least another visit next summer.

Mary Margaret has Bible School this week. She is the coordinator of the joint bible school of their church and St. Monica's Catholic. She seems very happy to be occupied in this way. When I had three little ones I was more home centered than church centered. But then I was probably expecting again and Dad was in service so I had my hands full surviving.

Dad's birthday is a week from Saturday. Hopefully I'll find something to keep me occupied. Though weekends are difficult as everyone is busy with their family activities and I haven't desired the Sr. citizens group yet.

Just received your letter, Ann. Glad things are going so well for you. Seems like you're having some happy times and I'm happy for you.

I made a lovely long dress before I went to Alaska. It will be ready if I do get a chance for a special occasion. I know I'm invited to a Christmas wedding . . .

Have a happy Anniversary. I'll think of you and your happy Wedding Day!

Love,
Mother

Fortunately, Mary got to experience a second "happy Wedding Day" herself, when she married long-time friend Robert Campen (1922–1994) in 1977. They were blessed with seventeen wonderful years together before he died from cancer. They traveled to Europe, visiting France and England, and made several trips to Hawaii. For many years, autumn in New England was an annual adventure.

I understand the blessings of a second marriage, because my dear Patrick and I were married in 2006. It was a special moment when I came across a treasured note written by my husband's mother, Helen Patrick Wirtz (1928–2015), a woman very close to my heart, as was her husband Jack (1921–2016). After she died, I discovered a sticky note she'd tucked into one of her Bibles, knowing one day I would find it. She wrote, *Ann, you are the best wife Pat could ever get. Helen.* It's now a sticky note tucked in my Bible.

A long letter or a simple note, what we write or say to each other can be deeply meaningful, even life changing. May our words be thoughtful and considerate, kind and compassionate, for their impact is rarely forgotten,[1] and kindness allows for all the unknowns of a person's situation.[2] As a child who loved to read, it was often frustrating when the main characters didn't "speak their mind," and, in my estimation, correct and solve the problems they faced or saw occurring. With maturity, I understand that while some things need to be carefully said, it is far wiser to take our words to the Lord in prayer first. He will guide us and handle every situation according to his will. In surrendering to him, *the peace of God, which surpasses all understanding, will guard your hearts and minds through Christ Jesus* (Philippians 4:7 NKJV).

[1] *Pleasant words are like a honeycomb,*
Sweetness to the soul and health to the bones (Proverbs 16:24 NKJV).

[2] *There is one who speaks rashly like the thrusts of a sword,*
But the tongue of the wise brings healing (Proverbs 12:18 NIV).

APRIL

CHAPTER 9 . . . A HERITAGE OF FAITH

My Family Connection to Pennsylvania, Virginia, and Kansas
Postcard: Arie Todd Greenleaf, 1997
Poem: "Plain Virtue" —About Great-Grandfather Noah Brubaker, 1994

CHAPTER 10 . . . A GIFT RECEIVED

My Connection to Irene Turner Wray and Arthena Wray Brubaker
Letter: Irene Turner Wray, 2008
Letter: Irene Turner Wray, 2011
Letter: Arthena Wray Brubaker, 2011

Chapter 9

A Heritage of Faith

My Family Connection to Pennsylvania, Virginia, and Kansas
Our son, Arie Todd Greenleaf, sent a postcard from Lancaster County,
Pennsylvania. His Brubaker ancestry lived there in the 1770s
and were men working the fields *as the Amish do today,*
as seen in the postcard picture.

LEARNING ABOUT ONE'S FAMILY history is intriguing for many reasons, primarily for the clues it gives to the personality and inclinations we inherit and ponder. Our gifts and talents, and even our peculiarities, are woven into our DNA, beautifully expressed in Psalm 139:13–16 NIV:

> *For you created my inmost being;*
>   *you knit me together in my mother's womb.*
> *14 I praise you because I am fearfully and wonderfully made;*
>   *your works are wonderful,*
>   *I know that full well.*
> *15 My frame was not hidden from you*
>   *when I was made in the secret place,*
>   *when I was woven together in the depths of the earth.*
> *16 Your eyes saw my unformed body;*
>   *all the days ordained for me were written in your book*
>   *before one of them came to be.*

Meeting distant family members whose faith, habits, and lifestyle revealed answers about myself changed my life. This family line is part of the American story, a story that began in Europe:

The family name *Brubaker* was first recorded in 1346 in the Canton of Zurich, Switzerland, on the eastern shore of Lake Zurich. One of the three earliest spellings was *Bruggbacher*, a variation meaning either *bridge-brook tender or a person living near the Brugg-Bach* (Brubaker, *Descendants of John and Anna*, A 12). The history of the Brubaker family is tied to the Swiss Anabaptist movement which began in 1525 in Zurich as part of the Protestant Reformation. The family embraced the tenets of the movement and experienced religious persecution. The reformers rejected infant baptism for believer's baptism and thus were called Anabaptists or "re-baptizers" for choosing to be "baptized again" as adults. They upheld the Bible as the source of religious authority and practice, and they believed in the separation of church and state. Eleven years later, Dutch Catholic priest Menno Simons (1496–1561) was baptized into the Swiss Anabaptist faith, and his influential leadership led to the movement's name, Mennonite.

Jakob Ammann (1644–1730) was a Swiss Anabaptist, a Mennonite elder from Bern, Switzerland. He believed the church needed to introduce *Meidung*, the German word meaning "to shun or avoid," which Ammann thought was the correct response toward individuals who had been excommunicated from the church. This led to a schism in 1693 and the formation of the Amish faith.

The third Anabaptist group was known as the German Baptist Brethren, also Dunkers or Dunkards, these names taken from the Pennsylvania German word *dunke*, which derives from "*tunken* meaning to dip or immerse." This refers to their triune baptism, face forward, done in the name of the Father, and the Son, and the Holy Ghost. Alexander Mack (1679–1735) baptized eight individuals in Schwarzenau, Germany, in 1708, forming The Brethren fellowship. Their beliefs were influenced by Pietism, a revival in Lutheranism, where followers sought a more meaningful faith involvement and believed life should be lived with a biblical emphasis on piety and holiness. Most Brethren churches descend from this group. A split in 1881 formed two main branches, the Church of the Brethren and the conservative Old German Baptist Brethren.

Our immigrant ancestor, John Brubaker (c.1750–1825), came to Lancaster County from the Palatinate along the Rhine River in Germany, where his ancestors fled to escape religious persecution in Switzerland. He joined others seeking the religious freedom they couldn't find in Europe, crossing the ocean to settle in the commonwealth of Pennsylvania, a haven for Quakers founded in 1681 by William Penn (1644–1718). Penn received the land from King Charles II (1630–1685) to settle a £ 16,000 debt the king owed to his late father, Admiral Sir William Penn (1621–1670). The commonwealth was named for the father and later became a haven, as well, for the three main Anabaptist groups, the Mennonite, Amish, and Brethren.

John Brubaker married Anna Myers (c.1750–1835) in 1774 in Cocalico Township in Lancaster County, and they had five children, their oldest is my third great-grandfather Henry (1775–1835). The family moved to Franklin County, Virginia, in 1789, where they lived for fifteen years before permanently settling in Botetourt, now part of Roanoke County, Virginia. Upon moving there, they left the Mennonite faith and joined the Brethren Church. Today, my Kansas second cousins are still members of the Old German Baptist Brethren Church, some now in the New Conference, maintaining the faith tradition our ancestors embraced not long after the end of the Revolutionary War (1783).

Many Brubakers stayed in Virginia, but some moved west. Great-Grandfather Noah Brubaker (1836–1917) left, going first to Clark County, Ohio, where he married Great-Grandmother Elizabeth Baird (1840–1926) in 1863. His first wife had died the year before, leaving behind their son. Noah continued moving west, the family living in Indiana, Illinois, Missouri, and Nebraska, their family of seven children, plus his first son, finally moving to Kansas in 1900.

. . . A Unique Sidenote: Patrick and I took a road trip to Roanoke in 2020, first stopping in nearby Wirtz, Virginia, where we took a picture standing by the Wirtz Road street sign. His family is not from there, but it was fun to discover this unincorporated community in Franklin County. Afterward, we drove to Roanoke to see where my ancestors lived and took a picture standing by the street sign, Brubaker Drive. Around the corner is the "Old Brubaker Cemetery." Pausing before the headstones and contemplating the lives of my "Greats" was deeply moving . . .

Postcard ~ Arie Todd Greenleaf, 1997

Front:
Pennsylvania
The postcard is a photograph of an Amish man managing a team
of four horses pulling a baler,
as two Amish men are stacking straw bales onto a low cart.
Back:
Pennsylvania
Horse-drawn farm equipment plays an important part in working
the Amish fields.
The Amish strive to live in harmony with nature
and their lifestyle has seen little change in 275 years.

March 28, 1997

A plain & simple lifestyle, but hard work from sunup to sundown.
I saw some Amish men working the fields just as in this picture.
A note from the road to say I love you,
Todd

Poem – Great-Grandfather Noah Brubaker, 1994

This poem speaks of the inspirational life and faith of my Great-Grandfather, as *he sought for bread to win*, true of farmers, then and now.

IRENE TURNER WRAY, MY second cousin and member of the Old German Baptist Brethren Church, shared this poem, a tender memory of our Great-Grandfather Noah Brubaker, who settled in Sawyer, Pratt County, Kansas in 1902. His inspirational legacy is one of persistence, hard work, and devout faith, a way of life still practiced by descendants who are farming the same land over a century later. Written by an unidentified cousin, the poem is dated January 31, 1994, and conveys the joy of a simple and faithful life.

> Plain Virtue
> From the mountains of Virginia
> To the sunbathed western plain;
> Grandpa's journey now has ended,
> But his mem'ries still remain.
>
> Grandsons sleeping in the sun room
> Grandpa's house so still at night;
> While the clock upon the mantel
> Chimed the hours 'til dawning light.
>
> Grandpa's stature was substantial
> To the lad who viewed him then;
> And his labors were impressive,
> As he sought for bread to win.

Many times while he was working,
I would watch him take his stride;
To the well-house 'neath the windmill,
Where the dipper hung inside.

Brushing back his drooping broad-brim,
Tipping dipper to his lips,
Let the water quench the parching,
Trickle down with eager sips.

I remember in the evening,
In the swing out by the fence;
How he rested and recounted,
And regaled with life's events.

So, the clock upon the mantel,
And the dipper by the tap,
And the swing out by the fencerow,
Bring me mem'ries of Grandpap.

But those things were only trinkets,
And they moldered through the years;
Though restored, they've lost their luster,
To the one who clearly hears . . .

Now, the chime of harp immortal;
And the water from the throne,
And the rest that's life eternal,
Bidding Grandpa, "Welcome home."

True, his feats were oft recounted,
And the tales repeated wide;
But the greatest of his virtues,
Was the faith in which he died.

Chapter 10

A Gift Received

My Connection to Irene Turner Wray and Arthena Wray Brubaker
These letters are from my second cousins from Sawyer, Kansas, a sweet
and sensitive sharing of life and gratitude for our *"Godly Heritage."*

WE WERE LIVING IN Northern Wisconsin again, the area we called home more than once after Arie and I honeymooned there in 1967. The year 2000 was ending, and the predicted doom that Y2K was to bring a year earlier at midnight with the transition from the twentieth to the twenty-first century had never materialized. So Arie encouraged me to fulfill a long-time desire and take the four-week genealogy class that was starting in January at Nicolet College in nearby Rhinelander. The decision to take the class and venture into the world of genealogical research has turned out to be more astonishing than I could ever have imagined, making it one of the most thrilling and profound adventures of my life. This journey of discovery led to meeting and visiting distant families, which included a visit to the farm in Hugoton, Kansas, where my father was raised.

When our class instructor said, "The fourth largest genealogical research center in the nation is housed three hours south in Madison, inside the Wisconsin Historical Society building on the Library Mall on the University of Wisconsin (UW) campus," I was ecstatic! Since our son was starting his senior year at UW, a trip was planned to see him and explore the family records available for research. I had no idea what I would find inside this venerable building, a campus landmark since 1900, but I would soon find out.

A vast and unknown world lay before me on that winter morning in 2001, when I visited the hallowed Historical Society building for the first time. Walking up the worn marble steps leading to the second-floor library and then up narrow wooden steps to the top floor of the building gave a rush of hopeful anticipation. Opening the door carefully, I stepped into a room filled with bookshelves holding one volume after another of family surnames. A quick search took me to the book that changed my life: *Descendants of John and Anna Myers Brubaker, 1750–1995* by Marwin E. Brubaker and Margaret Brubaker Eller. It was a breathtaking, unforgettable moment when I found my name. I was "hooked."

Once we were home, my husband located a telephone number for Margaret Eller, and we had a wonderful conversation. Her brother had sadly died, but their work had been completed before he passed. Researching and compiling their two-inch-thick, teal volume containing the historical and genealogical record of the Brubaker family had been an immense and comprehensive undertaking. I eagerly purchased one of her remaining books, an awe-inspiring tome. The journey had begun, with many trips back to Madison revealing more amazing facts about numerous family branches.

Toward the end of summer, my growing curiosity to see if any Brubakers still lived in Sawyer, where my father was born in 1910, prompted the logical next step in my genealogical adventure: a phone call to City Hall. The immediate response to my inquiry was a laugh and a resounding, "Yes!" Barbara Short, Sawyer City Clerk, faxed a page from the telephone book with individuals highlighted who turned out to be my second cousins, all of us descendants of Great-Grandparents Noah and Elizabeth. I called Donald, and thus began the most remarkable, loving, and satisfying aspect of my entire genealogical quest, getting to know my Kansas kin. The Brubaker family units are Donald (1929–2022) and Arthena (Wray) (1930–2017); his brother Joel "Joe" (1931–2023) and Lorraine (Eller) (1933–2018); and Irene Turner Wray (1920–2011) and her husband LaDrue Wray (1916–2007).

. . . A Descriptive Sidenote: My second cousins and their families are still Old German Baptist Brethren. In 1902 Noah and Elizabeth were among fifteen charter members of the church's Sand Creek District. Noah was ordained an Elder in 1906 at the annual Lovefeast, held that year in their barn, some of which is still standing. Their lifestyle resembles the Old

Order Mennonites and the Amish, except members drive cars and modern tractors and utilize electricity in their homes. Their clothing is the original modest design and honors the Old Way. Women wear lovely long dresses and prayer caps, and the men don broadfall pants and black, wide-brimmed hats. Worldly pleasures, including television and radio, are avoided, but they enjoy life immensely with a kind and good-hearted spirit . . .

Since our fathers were born five years apart in adjoining Kansas counties, Arie and I always talked about going to the Greenleaf Ranch in Kingman and then visiting my Brubaker cousins in Pratt. His terrible cancer diagnosis in 2003 and his passing a year later, however, kept that from happening. In November 2004 I honored our dream by flying to Wichita, Kansas, my birth city, the family farms located eighty miles west. Meeting my second cousins in person was a significant, even confounding experience, because I simply saw myself in them. Observing their ways and sensibilities was a personal revelation, providing valuable insight into my own personality. Staying with Donald and Arthena and meeting all the families opened a window on my draw to faith and my approach to life, demonstrating the reality of genetic inheritance. Donald and Arthena, Joe and Lorraine, and Irene and LaDrue are no longer with us—and how deeply they are missed—but knowing them has been a profound blessing, their loving friendships a tremendous gift!

Since I was recently widowed when we met, they were thrilled when Patrick and I married in 2006. The joy of being with these delightful people prompted our visit two years later in mid-October. We drove to Sawyer, and Patrick's heart knit with theirs, for he, too, was in awe of these precious, faithful Brubaker cousins, and they embraced him as their own. He especially enjoyed driving one of their large tractors and four wheeling down the straight country roads bordered by milo ready for harvesting and fields newly planted with winter wheat.

Saturday evening brought all the families to Joe and Lorraine's beautiful home to dine elegantly on linen and to relish her excellent dinner. The following morning found us worshipping together at their simple yet inspiring church service. Patrick and I sat in the middle of the congregation, the men on his side and the women on mine, all of us on the original wooden pews built in 1907 when the Meeting House was completed more than a century ago. A modern kitchen and restroom facilities have been added, but their original Meeting House remains a treasured and functional landmark. Completing this historic setting is the Pleasant View Cemetery, peacefully situated next to the building, where the headstones for Noah and Elizabeth are prominent, and where my second cousins are buried. The uplifting worship service gave eloquent testimony and insight into the Old German Baptist Brethren faith and was a tremendous experience.

The next morning, before leaving for North Carolina, we stopped at the lovely home of Donald's son Randy, a church elder. His dear wife, Carol, had prepared a hearty and delicious farm breakfast. With tears of gratitude, Patrick returned thanks before our meal, my own emotion matching his. In recalling the absolute joy from over twenty years of steady contact with my Kansas family, tears again fill my eyes. What if I'd not taken the 2001 genealogy class nor made my telephone call to Sawyer? To have never known the love and friendship of my dear second cousins is a stunning thought. Simply unthinkable!

Once we returned home, I wrote an article for *The Pratt Tribune*, published on Friday, November 14, 2008. It was titled "Reverence for Kansas Roots" and was an account of our trip to Sawyer. An excerpt about the music we sang at the worship service follows, with my closing thoughts taken from one of their songs:

> The music each Sunday is as distinctive as their dress. We sang from a pocket-sized hymnal titled "A Collection of Hymns and Sacred Songs." A minister reads one verse, a deacon starts the singing, and the people join in a cappella, the melody slow and the words clearly sung. This continued for each verse, the words a meaningful offering unto God . . . We were in love: with Kansas, the farms, the Brethren, and my own sweet family. One of the verses from their hymnal expresses our prayerful good-bye:
> *Peace to our brethren give;*
> *Fill all our hearts with love,*
> *In faith and patience may we live.*
> *And seek our rest above.*

Letter ~ Irene Turner Wray, 2008

12-13-08

Dear Ones:
   A note to you, the book "Chicken Soup for the Soul Christmas," I enjoyed your story, "Memories of a Christmas Doll"!
   Do you still have the doll?
   And Donald brought me a copy of the "Pratt Tribune" with your story of the trip to Ks. It was so interesting, and the travels of Noah Brubaker. I didn't remember them living in Neb.
   The integrity our forefathers had to move around with a family & etc. Makes us so Thankful for our "Godly Heritage."
   When I read the piece, brought tears to my eyes to be a part of the family on down through the ages. You have a way of expressing your thoughts, makes it so real.
   I enjoyed the treats you left with us, were really tasty with me tea!!
   We had a snow & windy day Tues, nice & sunny since. Temp 40↓. Glad you took time to stop in & to meet Patrick. Come again.
   Love,
   Irene & Dana [her daughter]

Letter ~ Irene Turner Wray, 2011

March/April 2011

Dear Ann and Patrick,

I received the book you sent me at Christmas time. Accept my apology for a late Thank You! for it. I have been reading "The Henderson Co. Curb Market."

You did have to do a lot of research to get it all-together, "God Bless" you for your efforts and time.

It was a nice surprise when I turned and saw your picture & related about the Brubaker families. I have memories going to western KS to visit them.

Doug & Randy [Donald and Arthena's sons] have some cattle on my wheat ground pasturing the wheat. I enjoy watching the cattle come to the water tank & hay bunk. And the chore boys come & go. We have had 0 degree weather this winter and then warmer & sunshine. We would like to see a good rain, dry here.

Congratulations on your Grandbaby / and she be having 1 yr old birthday. Grandbabies are precious!

We are missing Donald & Arthena. They left the 1st of Jan. for Fla.

This finds God Blessing me. I have some health problems but with Dr. visit I'm doing good. I do have macular degeneration of the eyes, that is a hindrance from doing sewing and can still read but tires my eyes. I have the Bible on C.D. so that passes time. "God is so good." I appreciate Dana with me, she is a help in caring for she does the cooking & etc.

Do have a house clean lady come in once a wk. A nurse from hospice comes out once a wk. to give me a shower, they are so helpful in other things. But I really appreciate Dana's care & companionship. She does sewing for herself, and another sister works at the library in Pratt one P.M. a wk. And LaDonna is a big help, she has a job in Pratt, but stops by to check on us and brings us Sun. lunch and spends P.M. Then the church family stop in for visits & usually a plate of cookies, etc.

We appreciate this.

Must close, hope you can read this—with my eyesight not good.

Our Love & "God's Blessings" to you,

Irene & Dana

Letter ~ Arthena Wray Brubaker, 2011

November 2011

Hello Ann and Patrick,
    Across the miles...
    We wished to call you, but haven't checked to locate your phone NO. We wanted to let you know <u>little</u> Irene Wray (75 lbs.) passed away in her sleep. She was so ready to go to Heaven—God has two dwellings, one in Heaven and the Other in a thankful heart.

    Two days ago, it looked sooo wintery (like snow) now it's beautiful days again—
    We think of you with Love and Prayers,
    Donald and Arthena
    God Bless you always

MAY

CHAPTER 11 . . . A LOVING SON

My Connection to Arie Todd Greenleaf
Letter: Charlotte Remick Brubaker, 1972
Inscription: Arie Todd Greenleaf, Mother's Day, 1993

CHAPTER 12 . . . A SOLDIER'S STORY

My Connection to Kenneth L. Brubaker Sr. and Charlotte Remick Brubaker
Letter: Kenneth Lee Brubaker, World War II, 1945

Chapter 11

A Loving Son

*My Connection to Arie Todd Greenleaf
This is a cherished Mother's Day inscription
about faith and love for the Lord.*

AFTER OUR HONEYMOON IN the Northwoods of Wisconsin, Arie and I dreamed of living there. When he took a job as a counselor at the local guidance center in Rhinelander in 1971, our dream came true. We made many friends and loved our life, especially when I became pregnant. Sadly, however, unforeseen circumstances occurred several months prior to our son's birth that would require a move from the community that had embraced us, and from the home we enjoyed on Midget Lake. We left two months after Arie Todd's birth. A letter from my encouraging mother, Charlotte Remick Brubaker (1910–2002), dated August 27, 1972, has been tucked away for over fifty years, the envelope marked *Save*. The following excerpt shares her response to the birth of her grandson a week earlier and to Arie's job loss:

> My dear Ann & Arie—
> It was surely nice to talk to you both. I had it in mind to call you Thurs. nite when Todd was 1 week old—but a neighbor came by, so I didn't get the call made. The weeks go by in a hurry and little Todd will grow fast. I'm glad you're feeling well, Ann.

Of course, we were so very sorry about your job, Arie. You have to think things happen for the best—tho' it's hard to justify what has happened. There may be some professional jealousy on [his boss's] part. I just can't understand his thinking, unless he feels, Arie, you are surpassing him in the contacts you've successfully made. The publicity and all you've gotten certainly attests to the fact you have done a good job.

Much easier to talk the situation over face to face, so will really be glad to have you come see us. And what's important to me—I'll get to see little Todd. In the meantime, we pray the job for which you were interviewed will come thru . . . Keep up your spirits. So thankful for your friends, who can help you in this respect. God Bless you. Love always,
Mom

There are moments in life we never forget, and giving birth to our son will always be one of the most joyous ones. However, the opposite emotion occurred the day after he was born. Arie was walking up the hospital sidewalk to visit us when I glanced out the window and saw him. Deep hurt, fear, and sadness from the job loss and all the resultant uncertainty overwhelmed me. However, I was determined not to despair in front of him. With the sliver of hope from the upcoming job interview plus the healthy birth of our son tamping down the anxiety, I put on a smile.

In preparation for Arie Todd's delivery, the 1965 publication, seventh edition of *Thank You, Dr. Lamaze* by Marjorie Karmel, was a must read. First published in 1959, Karmel revolutionized pregnancy through her personal journey to discover *the deeply satisfying experience of painless childbirth*. Her fascinating story encourages women to be active, not passive, participants in the birth of their children through education, and through the breathing and exercise techniques developed by Dr. Fernand Lamaze to help in the birthing process. My worn and well-read volume is still in my possession, along with the 1967 companion book, *Six Practical Lessons for an Easier Childbirth* by Elisabeth Bing, R.P.T. Her book promotes the Lamaze method and was a great help in learning how to give birth naturally. Bing dedicated her book *to all the young parents who have studied with me, and to the memory of Marjorie Karmel.* Bing worked with Karmel, and in 1960 they founded the not-for-profit organization which became Lamaze International. (Karmel, a professional actress and best-selling author with *Thank You, Dr. Lamaze*, died tragically in 1964.)

Preparation also included taking the class on natural childbirth taught by a good friend, where Arie learned how to be a partner and coach through the labor process. Dr. Marvin Wright, my OB/GYN, was nearing retirement and was uncertain about natural childbirth, but he was still willing to give the Lamaze method a try, making me his first patient. Although it turned out to be harder than I anticipated, breathing control and knowledge were definite helps, and I'm forever grateful I could deliver our son using this method. Since hospitals were beginning to allow husbands in the delivery room, and I knew St. Mary's Hospital would eventually allow it, too, I eagerly made that suggestion, but in 1972 that was a step too far for both the doctor and my husband.

The job interview went well, and Arie was hired for a counseling position at a center in Trempealeau County, Wisconsin, three hours southwest of Rhinelander. We moved into our home in nearby Whitehall on Halloween. Our longing for the beloved North Woods never abated, however, and after a year and a half, we moved to Minocqua and started The Greenleaf Shoppe. This was a foreshadowing of our son's childhood, even through college, for we moved many times. My best explanation for our peripatetic life is that each decision was either necessary or made sense to us, especially later in life once we started our business Rapture Inc. and could choose where we wanted to live.

Along with Illinois and Wisconsin, we also experienced the joy of living in Missouri, Indiana, and in both North and South Carolina. Our longest stint was six years in Arbor Vitae, Wisconsin, before moving to North Carolina in 2002. We bought a cranberry-colored house on Davis Mountain in Hendersonville, saying it would be our last home until heaven. And for Arie, it was. After marrying my dear Patrick, a Hendersonville native, I'm thankfully still here.

Through all the changes, "Todd," as we called him during his growing up years, managed the moves. It helped that some were local, and he was in the same elementary and junior high schools in Bloomington, Illinois. After graduating from the University of Wisconsin and acquiring his M Ed from Clemson University and his PhD from the University of Iowa, he began his counseling career. He taught at the University of Arkansas and was at Seattle University for nine years. He and his lovely wife Dewa Shrestha (who was born in Kathmandu, Nepal, and grew up in Madison, Wisconsin) and their two children, Divya and Aarush, our adorable grands, are my greatest blessings. Currently, my son is a Professor in the Department of

Counseling in the College of Psychology at Nova Southeastern University in Ft. Lauderdale, Florida.

Six months prior to Arie Todd's 1993 Mother's Day message, we moved to Brown County Indiana. We set up our fledgling pewter jewelry business in a barn on the property we were able to purchase on land contract. We hung blankets to insulate an area warmed by a space heater. A week later, we attended a Christian Camping International (CCI) Conference in Nashville, Tennessee, our foray into a world where our jewelry could hopefully find a niche. That previous summer we successfully made camp logos and attached them to necklaces and keychains to be sold to campers. Our first ones were for Camp Lurecrest in Lake Lure, North Carolina, not too far from where I live today.

We sold enough jewelry that summer we felt our business had a future, so after much prayer, it was clear Arie needed my full-time help, requiring my resignation from the best job I ever had. After two wonderfully rewarding years as an Assistant Administrator and Reading Specialist at Camperdown Academy, a private school for children with dyslexia in Greenville, South Carolina, leaving was very difficult. Nevertheless, it was the right decision. Once again, we were living on faith, hope, and prayer to meet our needs as we sought to develop and grow Rapture Inc.

The CCI Conference was encouraging despite a very slow start. Midmorning that first day, I was overcome with fear and had to step behind the partition for a quick prayer. Our steady income had ended, we had just moved into our home, and looming before us were the financial responsibilities that were depending on the success of our infant business. Mercifully, the Lord spoke to my anxious heart saying, "You don't know what will happen in the next few minutes, but I do. Trust me." And I did. It was a humbling, never-to-be-forgotten lesson when a woman from a Christian camp in California soon stopped at our booth and ordered jewelry for the next summer season, seven months away. Miraculously, but God knew, she wrote a check for the full amount, her kindness helping us get further down this "unknown road," one we would travel for twelve astonishing years, the essence of our experience captured in Isaiah 42:16 NKJV:

> *I will bring the blind by a way they did not know;*
> *I will lead them in paths they have not known.*
> *I will make darkness light before them,*
> *And crooked places straight.*
> *These things I will do for them,*

And not forsake them.

He was with us from beginning to end, all to God's Glory!

Inscription ~ Arie Todd Greenleaf, 1993

May 9, 1993
Happy Mother's Day!

> "The happiest heart that ever beat
> Was in some quiet breast
> That found the common daylight sweet,
> And left to heaven the rest."
>
> —Cheney

I pray that this can be true of you. Your life has been an example to me, through your Faith and Love for the Lord. Always remember that through whatever circumstances you go through that the Lord loves you and He is still on His throne. Praise Him, for the Lord is Good!

I love you <u>very</u> much,
Todd

ARIE TODD WROTE THIS inscription on the inside of his Mother's Day gift, a beautiful version of *Mr. Jones, Meet the Master, Sermons and Prayers of Peter Marshall*, edited by Catherine Marshall and published in 1950. He purchased this book at our favorite shop in Nashville, Indiana, the used bookstore, where every visit was an enticement to acquire one more literary treasure for our library.

Chapter 12

A Soldier's Story

*My Connection to Kenneth L. Brubaker Sr.
and Charlotte Remick Brubaker
My father's remarkable World War II letter from 1945 inspired this
book, a profound mid-western account, eloquent in its simplicity,
historic truth, and the clear realization that war is really hell.*

My parents were married in 1936 and had three children. I was their only girl, the middle child between Ken Jr. and Peter. They were wonderful parents and are extremely dear to me. Attempting to describe them brings tears, for the depth of my love and gratitude is beyond description. Perhaps the best summation is to thank God they were my parents, and to acknowledge how their love and encouragement made a tremendous foundation for my life. To their core, my parents were kind, loving, sympathetic, generous, hard-working and disciplined in their tasks, with a steady commitment to each other and to their family.

They were born in Kansas in 1910, my father on the farm in rural Sawyer, and my mother in upscale Manhattan, with KSAC exerting a sophisticated influence. Wichita was home when I made my appearance in 1948, but a job-transfer with the Dixie Cup Company took us to the St. Louis area three months later. Family life had its normal challenges, of course, because nothing is perfect, but it is clear we had a blessed childhood. My middle-class Missouri upbringing, which I assumed everyone experienced, had a joy to it that has become magnified over the years. With the First United Methodist Church on the corner from our house, and our schools within walking distance: Avery Elementary, Plymouth Junior High, and Webster Groves Senior High, life was lived within a wholesome and comforting environment. Our community provided a strong academic program along with all the opportunities available in the St. Louis area in the 1950s and 1960s, so, as children, we received the proverbial "roots and wings."

My father was raised on their winter wheat farm in Hugoton, located in southwestern Kansas, where his family settled in 1916. His older brother, Bernard, stayed on the farm, but Dad chose to pursue a degree and career in business and headed to Manhattan to attend Kansas State College (1931 name change), where he met Mom. They were both members of a Greek society, Mom thoroughly enjoying the Delta Delta Delta sorority, and Dad a proud member of the Alpha Tau Omega fraternity.

Mom graduated with a degree in Physical Education in 1932, and Dad was slated to graduate in 1935 with a degree in Commerce but was unable to finish. Although he didn't graduate from college, my father became highly successful as the St. Louis District Sales Manager for the Dixie Cup Company, which merged with the American Can Company in 1957. We grew up with Dad's Dixie Cups and Mom's P.E.O., the Philanthropic Educational Organization she joined in 1932. Her mother, my Grandmother Harriet, joined P.E.O. in 1929, and I joined Chapter BC in Hendersonville, North Carolina, in 2023. We saw first-hand and were influenced by the fruit of our parents' commitments.

After twenty-five exemplary years in sales, Dad retired when his health began to deteriorate. He was sadly diagnosed with lung cancer and died in January 1973. His retirement party was held on May 30, 1972, at the Tan-Tar-A Resort in Osage Beach, Missouri. I compiled a scrapbook of pictures and the many cards and letters received from that very special day, every word of gratitude conveying deep respect, honor, and admiration for how capable and considerate my father was. Some of the letters are especially poignant. Meaningful excerpts that capture the essence of my father and his generation are proudly and gratefully shared:

> When I think of Ken Brubaker, I also think of the year of our last "National Dixie Cup Sales Meeting" in Atlantic City, New Jersey when Ken Brubaker was selected and honored as the Outstanding

Salesman of the Dixie Cup Company for the year 1950 . . . Your performance and achievements, Ken, have truly been outstanding and one only has to read the letter from Joe Aubuchon [President of Royal Papers Inc.] to know why you have been known as 'Mr. St. Louis' . . . You are still best known for being THE MAN. For you tackled problems head on . . . your courage in standing by convictions whether dealing with [individuals] or National Sales Directors.
—Rex S., American Can Company, Kansas City Sales Office, Overland Park, Kansas

. . . for me personally, one of the real satisfactions was having had the chance to work under your great leadership for over two years. Many districts had their troubles working together, but that was never the situation in Ken Brubaker's St. Louis District. You showed everyone how enjoyable it could be working together, at the same time our combined sales reached new heights . . . Personally, I had more respect for you as a man, and confidence in your leadership than anyone I have had the pleasure of working for, and that includes some pretty great people.
—Gary S., American Can Company, Kansas City Sales Office, Overland Park, Kansas

Thank you for your friendship, your guidance and your patience. Like so many of those who are there with you tonight, as well as those scattered across the country, we all owe you a portion of any of our present, or future success. Consequently, Ken, you may be retiring to the good life, but the Brubaker method will still be in service. Your techniques and philosophies are the cornerstone of our success.
—Bob C., American Can Company, Los Angeles, California

It is difficult to write this letter. How can you in mere words express heartfelt emotions of sadness and joy! It is not easy: it is so mixed with opposite feeling . . . I am so happy about your retirement. I can honestly say of all the mill men I know no one has earned it more! . . . With the joy, however, there is the tinge of sadness. It means that no longer will you call us regularly . . . I can no longer count on your sound advice to help in a problem. Yes, it will be strange not to have you active in the market and I do not like it . . . I console myself though it is merely a separation, and I am sure, knowing you as I do, you will continue to visit old friends. We then still can keep in touch. That is really a source of consolation. So,

Ken, with every good wish and a heartfelt prayer that God blesses you with a happy retirement!
—Sincerely, ROYAL PAPERS, INC., Joseph A., President

I have been actively associated with Ken Brubaker in the American Can Co. business for the last five years. Of this association, I am extremely proud, and it has been my privilege to know him as a man and gentleman, in every other phase of life. Throughout all our personal contacts, he has enriched my life, and although we are happy for him in his retirement, he will be greatly missed by the entire AMERICAN CAN CO. I feel something different about Ken's retirement, in that it is the passing of the era of a Generation. An Era of Wisdom, Knowledge, Morals, Stability, Honesty, Integrity, and caring for their Fellow Man. Kenny Brubaker does care for his Fellowman. I thank him for all that he has done for me in the past and wish him GOOD LUCK and Happiness in his retirement. God Love Him.
—Albert T., American Can Company, Des Moines, Iowa

After Dad died, it was several years before my mother had an opportunity to share these letters with me to keep and preserve. This occurred on a visit to her new home in Leisure World in Laguna Woods, California, where she moved to be near her sister, my dear Aunt Agnes Hacker (1905–1999). Their emotional and eloquent messages are astounding, and I responded then, as now, with tears of gratitude for my father, thankful he received these accolades before he died. The devastating thought: What if I'd never read them?! Their generation rarely, if ever, talked about their accomplishments, including their World War II experiences. Fortunately, these letters are available to reveal the heart, faith, and character of our common American story. They express the importance of respect, kindness, and consideration, and how *caring for our Fellow Man* advances the dreams and endeavors of every person. It is something to emulate again.

Albert's stirring description of my father encapsulates why the people of that era are called The Greatest Generation. They possessed traits honed by the ravages of the Great Depression in the 1930s and strengthened by the rigors of World War II in the 1940s. They were The Greatest Generation because they rose above their circumstances through the determination to do their duty, and through sacrifice, hard work, and faith, expected responses which flourished in simpler, though extremely challenging times.

My father served in the Army during World War II, and in March 1943 was sent to Camp Campbell, Kentucky, assigned to *Combat Command*

"A," the 9th *Tank Battalion*, the 20th *Armored Division*, with the rank of *Tec4*. He once said it was his ability to drive a tractor that led to his placement in the tank division. Indeed, Dad, along with many other soldiers, exchanged the family tractor for what he labels in one of his photographs *"Nightcap"*— *Gen. Sherman, 76 mm gun*, the vehicle that transported the Army across Europe. After the war, a colorful map and a letter of gratitude dated 4 July 1945 was sent from *C.M. Daly, Brigadier General, U.S. Army, Commanding* to the soldiers of Dad's division. The map highlights their route from Camp Campbell to Salzburg, Austria, their concluding location. Dates printed in red, along with notations of events and encounters, tell the story:

> DEPARTED Camp Campbell, 19 Jan 45
> ARRIVED Le Havre, France, 18 Feb 45 (Dad wrote the 17th.)
> DISEMBARKED and FIRST VIEW OF RUINS, 19 Feb 45
> CROSSED the Rhine River:
> HODGES MEMORIAL BRIDGE (PONTOON BRIDGE), 10 Apr 45
> EXTERMINATION CAMP FOUND, DACHAU, 29 Apr 45
> ARRIVED Salzburg, 04 May 45
> DIRECTED TO CEASE HOSTILITIES, 05 May 45
> OFFICIAL JOINT ANNOUNCEMENT FOR END OF THE WAR, 09 May 45.

The letter and map are included in my father's frayed and worn wartime album, a photographic wonderment. Dad identified and recorded the people, equipment, and locations seen in the small black and white photographs. There are many snapshots of his prized tank, which he also labeled *The original issue—Gen. Sherman*. However, the first picture in the album is the most important, for it shows five men proudly, yet casually, positioned around their tank and identified as *The Crew—O'Brian, Atkinson, Sheff, Jacques, Brubaker*.

When Mom moved to Leisure World in 1977, we had great fun driving her car across America, an almost two-thousand-mile trip on famed Route 66, all the way from St. Louis to Laguna Woods. Once there, we stayed with Aunt Agnes for a few days until Mom's home was ready, pure joy for this niece who dearly loved her aunt. Before flying home, Agnes called me into her bedroom and handed me a pale blue, tissue-paper-thin envelope outlined with red and blue parallelograms, the words VIA AIR MAIL imprinted beneath the missing stamp. The letter was from my dad, *Sgt. K.L. Brubaker*, and was addressed to my aunt and uncle, *Mr. & Mrs. James Hacker*, with the word *Save* underlined twice in the lower right corner. When Agnes and Jim received the letter in 1945, they immediately recognized its historic value and tucked it away for later. She released this archival masterpiece into my keeping, which I'm now honored to share.

Letter ~ Kenneth L. Brubaker, 1945

Germany
May-22-45

Dear Jim, Agnes, & Kiddies,

Thanks a million for the pocket knife, very thoughtful of you and something that will come in handy. Also, for the very nice letter which arrived only about four or five days ahead of the package.

Charlotte, in one of her letters had included a picture of all of you and Dick and Charlotte Sundeen. As you say, Agnes, your family is quickly growing up. Certainly doesn't seem possible C. Ann [daughter Charolotte Ann] and Jimmy should be the size the photo showed them to be.

I too think it is just swell that Charlotte and Kenny [son Ken Jr. 1942] are now near enough to all of you that you will be able to see one another before too long. Probably much quicker than I will. As yet we haven't the slightest idea as to what we will be doing in the near future. One day the rumor is "The Golden Gate in '48" and the next that we will be stationed over here. If the truth was really known, doubt if anyone knows for sure yet. The old Army saying of "it all depends upon the situation," covers it pretty well I think.

Well so far the year of '45 has been quite a year for this chicken to say the least. Now that it is all over we can tell you folks back home a lot more than was possible before they quit censoring our letters. We sailed from Boston Harbor on a pleasure liner named The Brazil Feb. 6th, and arrived at La Harve (*sic*), France Feb. 17th. The Ship wasn't too large and was quite crowded to say the least but the trip over wasn't too rough, at least I didn't get seasick tho a lot of the fellows did. We came over with a large convoy which also had our tanks along. The last two days at sea and one night the destroyer escorts were dropping depth charges all over the place, tho what they were after and if they succeeded we never found out.

La Harve was the first war torn place most of us had ever actually seen, and it was a good one. The Army, Navy, and particularly the Air Corp had really worked the place over. We didn't stay at La Harve any longer that it took to load up our trucks and moved on into a little French town near Rouen by the name of [uncertain]. Rouen, I believe, is France's fourth city and the birthplace of Joan of Arc. Quite a place, very old and just seeping with history and tradition. It too tho was pretty badly bombed and shelled in spots. The British and Canadians had fought down through there after their breakthrough at Caen. Around there we saw a lot of wrecked equipment both Jerry and ours, and a lot of graves. Some pretty heavy fighting was quite evident. It took us about a month to get our tanks cleaned up and combat stowed and then we started on our way for Germany. Easter Sunday found us well on our way on a trip that took four days and parts of three nights of pretty steady driving of these 30,000 ton jobs.

Some time I'll show you on a map the route we took, but some of the cities we roared and rumbled through were Amiens & Mons, France, Siege, Belgium, [uncertain, perhaps Maastricht] or something like that, Holland, and finally to our first stop in Germany, Alsdorf. This place was right on the edge of the then Ruhr Pocket, about 12 kilometers north of Aachen. That was the first time most of us had the chance to see and hear the big guns, boy they were really at it with tooth and toenail. We stayed there about a week and then moved Southeast to the southern edge of the pocket just north of Frankford. We crossed the Rhine at Bonn about 2 in the morning. Couldn't see too much of it except that it looked plenty wide, deep and swift. Crossed over on a pontoon bridge which is quite a thrill with a tank. We were to move into the pocket but before we got the march order the pocket collapsed so the only part of the outfit that got into that show was part of our military. We then got orders to get ready to move to Kassell which is about 70 miles S.W. of Berlin but about 3 hours before we pulled out that was changed because the Germans were trying to move large forces south into the mountains of Southern Germany, so we did likewise.

We started for Nuremberg leaving the First Army to join up with the 3rd. By the time we arrived near there Patton had things well under control, but the 7th Army further south had run into plenty of trouble, so we joined up with them on the move to Lake Munich. From there on business really picked up for us. Folks, it's a business that is hard to describe, for me anyway. I don't mind tieing (sic) into the Kraut Soldier, for after all that is what we mainly got into this for. But when you move into a burning town throwing everything you have at it, and besides a lot of Kraut soldiers you see little kids the size of Kenny Lee on up, scared to death and trying to get out of the way, you then realize that war is really hell. My earnest hope is that the American mothers and kiddies never, never have to go through anything like it. It's strictly no good.

Our outfit spear headed the drive into Munich along with two infantry divisions. Parts of our outfit had plenty of trouble with the 88's & Tigers, we had our share but came through O.K. Still driving number four tank of the first platoon, which in tank warfare is also number one tank of the second section. The sections take turns in leading and when we hit Munich it happened to be our turn. The Heinies were waiting for us, but by some hook or crook we out foxed them, got the drop on them and they really gave up in droves. We stayed in Munich just that night, and since a city street isn't too good a place to maneuver a tank, we turned the rest of it over to the infantry and we moved southeast headed for Salzburg, Austria. Had a little trouble every now and then along the way but the "Supermen" were surrendering with less effort each time we moved in on them. It was quite evident the end wasn't too far off.

One loses all track of the days and dates while moving like we did for we were hardly ever halted more than four or five hours at a time, but I believe it was the fifth of May when we took over Salzburg which was as far as we went. When we pulled in, I just happened to notice the mileage on the speedometer and if it was the fifth we had come 1000.4 miles in a month and four days. Quite a little trip in a tank, and when you have been driving it most all the way you really knew you had been places. Ever since then, except to move back across the river into Germany, we have just been fooling around, sleeping, and trying to get cleaned back up again. Boy, we were all a grimy bunch, and I am not fooling.

Salzburg is only 12 miles north of Hitler's Berchtesgaden here in the Austrian alps. As yet I haven't gotten over to see the place but want to before we leave this section. Germany as a whole is a very beautiful country, just like one big golf course and where we are now, which is just at the base of the Alps the scenery is really something for the book. Course these so's & so's just had 15 million slave laborers to keep things looking like a garden. There is really a job ahead of someone getting all these people rounded up and sent back home. They are of all sizes, shapes, and colors. The Russians, to me are the only ones that don't act as tho they are completely beaten.

We were the first ones to hit Hitler's most dreaded Concentration Camp which was right north of Munich called Dachau. Folks, there is no way of describing that place. There were 32,000 prisoners there, more dead than alive and on one railroad siding there were 39 box cars with an average of 50 bodies on each one, some more, some less. You could smell the place easily 10 miles away. Where the Heinies were going to take the bodies I have no idea. But after seeing things like that one really realizes what an unhuman, ruthless, nasty bunch these monkies are. The S.S. guards were really taken care of at Dachau by the American soldiers in one big way. If anything the taking care lasted too shortly. Anything was too good for those birds.

Needless to say we are all glad it is over over here and wished we could say the same for the Pacific. It will be a great day when things have settled back to normal again. I for one will be plenty tickled to be with the wife and son again.

Well folks 'tis past bedtime so will sign off.

Hope all of you are well. Personally I feel like a million. This rugged life in one sense of the word is quite the thing for an old "35 year older" I guess. Ha.

Bye for now with love to all of you,
Ken

Copies of my father's remarkable World War II letter have been shared with several organizations preserving the history of the war. A copy was also sent to the United States Holocaust Memorial Museum in Washington, DC. Rebecca L. Erbelding, Archivist, responded with a letter dated May 23, 2007. She made several intriguing observations including, *I found the letter very interesting—especially that he mentions the "summary justice" that the liberators enacted upon the SS guards they found. Most don't mention that... Since so many people still deny the Holocaust ever happened, we try to only collect original materials, so there is no way to accuse us of manipulating the documents.* The copy I sent was to be kept in their staff research files.

The United States Holocaust Memorial Museum and the US Army's Center of Military History joined together in 1985 to recognize the 20th Armored Division as a "liberating unit" identified as *Liberators*. On April 28, 1996, the 20th Armored Veterans Memorial Committee placed a bronze plaque showing the *Liberators* patch and an inscription in the archway at the entrance to the Dachau Concentration Camp. The English, French, and German text reads:

> IN HONOR OF THE 20th ARMORED DIVISION (LIBERATORS)
> U.S. 7th ARMY WHO PARTICIPATED IN THE LIBERATION
> OF DACHAU CONCENTRATION CAMP
> APRIL 29, 1945 AND IN EVERLASTING
> MEMORY OF THE VICTIMS OF NAZI BARBARISM,
> THIS TABLET IS DEDICATED APRIL 28, 1996
>
> 20th ARMORED DIVISION (LIBERATORS)
> VETERANS MEMORIAL COMMITTEE

The 1985 honor was conferred twelve years after my father died. The 1996 recognition is valuable because it records the facts of a terrible World War II reality. While Dad would have been pleased with the honor, I know he would have seen the military response as simply soldiers doing their job, and in doing so, they stumbled across an unspeakable atrocity. He had a duty and a responsibility to meet every challenge with determination and his best effort, and that is what he did. After all, he was a member of The Greatest Generation, but he will forever be my Dear Dad, a pragmatic Kansan who met life matter-of-factly with kindness, humor, and resolve, those genetics deep in his bones. No daughter could ever be more grateful, proud, or loved.

JUNE

CHAPTER 13 ... MATH AND THE SPACE RACE

My Connection to Rosina Shepardson, Lois Spano, and Winston Ragon
Letter: Winston Ragon, 1972

CHAPTER 14 ... GOOD FRIENDS

My Connection to Mary Bewig Vermillon and "Steph Dilly," Daughter of Phyllis Diller
Yearbook Messages: Mary Bewig Vermillon, 1963, 1964; Stephanie Diller, 1963, 1964

CHAPTER 15 ... THE PRESIDENT KENNEDY ERA

My Connection to Gail Monroe Crosson and the Peace Corps
Peace Corps Reminiscence: Gail Monroe Crosson, 2025

CHAPTER 16 ... TELEVISION TELLS A STORY

My Connection to *Sixteen in Webster Groves*
High School Reunion Booklets: *THE SPIRIT OF '66*, 1976; *WG 66 Class Reunion 86*, 1986

CHAPTER 17 ... TOO SOON AN ENDING

My Connection to Carol Shankland Kennedy Porter
Letter: Carol Shankland Kennedy, 1976

Chapter 13

Math and the Space Race

My Connection to Rosina Shepardson, Lois Spano, and Winston Ragon
Teachers instill unforgettable memories, the hard ones soften over time, and the others stand bright, both challenging us to be the best *we can be.*

THE CORNER OF EAST Lockwood and Plymouth Avenues in Webster Groves was the site chosen for the location of the brand-new Plymouth Junior High School. The building was designed to accommodate the explosion of children born after World War II who became identified as the Baby Boomer Generation (1946–1964). Across the country, we were the largest number of children to ever enter the school system, challenging school administrators everywhere to accommodate this increased enrollment. There were so many upcoming students in our community, Steger Junior High across town in Rock Hill was also built. In September 1960, these two schools along with Hixson Junior High, located near the football field where the high school games are played, welcomed those entering the seventh, eighth, and ninth grades. It was sad saying good-bye to Avery School, because those elementary years were golden, yet it was exciting to move forward. We entered Plymouth Junior High with great anticipation and became the first class to attend all three years before starting tenth grade at Webster Groves Senior High School, located just around the corner at 100 Selma Avenue.

JUNE

Memories abound about those junior high years when "We are the Patriots!" became our resounding cry, a backdrop to our adjustment to having lockers, homeroom, and different teachers for every subject. Our enthusiasm supported plays and assemblies, and our school spirit was notched up for thrilling football and basketball games. Going to my first "Dance" was a bit fearful, but moving my upper torso in the opposite direction of my hips and legs to imitate Chubby Checker moving to his song, "The Twist," along with just being with friends, made the evening fun. The boyfriend-girlfriend dimension became something to navigate, but friendships were formed that have lasted a lifetime.

The junior high years coincided with the Space Race between the United States and the Soviet Union, which seriously began after Russia launched Sputnik 1 on October 4, 1957. About the size of a beach ball, Sputnik was the first artificial satellite to orbit the earth, which it did successfully every 98 minutes for three weeks, until its three radio batteries were depleted. Watching Sputnik streak across the night sky as it sent its signal to earth brought great consternation and fear. Everyone wondered about the negative consequences that would result from this achievement. *October Sky* by Homer Hickam Jr. is one of my favorite books and a wonderful movie. Originally published in 1998 under the title *Rocket Boys*, this fascinating account tells the story of Hickam's coal mining family in Coalwood, West Virginia, and the inspiration Sputnik 1 gave him as a teenager to build a rocket despite opposition from his father, who wanted him to embrace coal mining for his future. The book vividly portrays America's hostile and inspired reaction to Russia's achievement. The success of Sputnik 1 made clear the United States had some serious catching up to do. Under the leadership of President Dwight D. Eisenhower, the first major step began when Congress created the National Aeronautics and Space Administration (NASA) in 1958. Homer Hickam Jr. was able to fulfill his childhood aspiration when he became a NASA engineer years later, demonstrating the power of a dream.

America forged ahead with great gusto and ultimately won the Space Race. President John F. Kennedy (1917–1963) set the bar high through his exhortation to America to go to the moon. His passionate address at Rice University, September 12, 1962, is firm and persuasive for any challenge:

> We choose to go to the moon. We choose to go to the moon in this decade and do the other things, not because they are easy, but because they are hard, because that goal will serve to organize

and measure the best of our energies and skills, because that challenge is one that we are willing to accept, one we are unwilling to postpone, and one which we intend to win.

America did win on July 20, 1969, when Neil Armstrong (1930–2012), Commander of Apollo 11, became the first man to step on the moon, his message concise and profound, "One small step for man, one giant leap for mankind." Edwin "Buzz" Aldrin (1930–), the Lunar Module Pilot, followed him declaring, "Beautiful view. Magnificent desolation." Michael Collins (1930–2021) was the Command Module Pilot orbiting the moon for twenty-one and a half hours until the astronauts had completed their mission on the moon's surface. They rendezvoused in space and splashed down in the Pacific Ocean on July 24, unleashing an enormous, world-wide celebration.

Before this tremendous achievement could be realized, however, much had to be accomplished. America had to first launch a man, and later a woman, into space and then return them safely back to earth. On April 9, 1959, NASA introduced the seven men chosen to become the original Mercury 7 astronauts (Astro is Greek for stars): Scott Carpenter, Gordon Cooper, John Glenn, Gus Grissom, Wally Schirra, Alan Shepard, and Deke Slayton. Their stories have forever fascinated, with many books written to give a glimpse into their lives and the Space Race that dominated the late 1950s and the 1960s. Tom Wolfe's riveting, epic account, *The Right Stuff*, published in 1979 and adapted to film in 1983, is the most famous. An excellent companion book, *The Astronaut Wives Club* by Lily Koppel, was published in 2013. Koppel interviewed some of the wives of "The Original Seven" astronauts, as well as several of the wives of the astronauts who followed and presents their compelling stories. Her book is an honest, thoughtful account of how the wives and families coped with and survived, for the most part, the demands, pressures, and losses of the early space years. She reveals both sides of this tremendous American Adventure, the glory and the heartache.

My ongoing fascination with the history of the Space Race began in earnest on May 5, 1961, at 9:34 a.m. EST, or about 8:30 a.m. in the Midwest, when I listened to the classroom PA system broadcast the launch of Astronaut Alan Shepard (1923–1998) as he became the first American and second man into space. The first man was Soviet Cosmonaut Yuri Gagarin (Cosmo is Greek for space) who orbited the earth once on April 12, 1961, his flight lasting 108 minutes. Less than a month later, Alan Shepard piloted the Mercury spacecraft *Freedom 7* on a suborbital, 115-mile altitude flight that traveled 302 miles, totaling fifteen minutes. Ten years later, Shepard commanded *Apollo 14*, becoming the fifth and oldest U.S. astronaut at age forty-seven to fly into space and walk on the moon, where he was also the first to hit a golf shot on the lunar surface. Through the wonders of genealogical research, I uncovered an astonishing connection with Alan Shepard, something completely unthinkable as a child, and surprising as an adult. We have the same eighth Great-Grandparents, Thomas Bradbury (1610/11–1694/95) and Mary Perkins (1615–1700), making us ninth cousins.

The launch on May 5, 1961, took place during Miss Rosina Shepardson's seventh-grade math class. I joined in the countdown, marveling as the liftoff sent Shepard into space. This historic and thrilling accomplishment has stayed with me to this day, a highlight of my junior high years. As never-to-be-forgotten as this event was, however, simply being in Miss Shepardson's class has also been unforgettable, for different reasons. My clear memories center on her appearance and on my struggle with word problems. Her long, salt-and-pepper hair was braided into a coronet circling her head, giving height to her small frame. She may have seemed the quintessential "old maid" to a student, but her story would be fascinating to know from an adult perspective.

Math has always posed a bit of a dilemma. Learning arithmetic operations was easy enough, but the minute words were attached to numbers, and it had to be determined which process to use to solve a math problem, I was sunk. I have no doubt my issue with solving word problems frustrated Miss Shepardson to no end. My seventh-grade report card states, *Tests not up to standard at all.* The next year was no better, for in October she wrote, *Ann's test was very poor.* And it got worse, because I missed a week of school in December. My family and I drove Route 66 to Phoenix, Arizona, to see my beloved Brubaker grandparents, and then onto Los Angeles, California, to spend Christmas with my dear Aunt Agnes and Uncle Jim. Miss Shepardson wrote in my January "Student's Progress Report," *Both tests very poor. Ann hasn't seemed to have 'been here' as usual. Could that week off have affected her so she lost contact?"* My March report states, *Test unsatisfactory, daily work 'erratic.'*

Yes, *erratic* sums up my junior high math classes, but fortunately, and surprisingly, Miss Shepardson gave me a C+ for my final report each year, and I managed a C+ in Algebra from my ninth-grade math teacher, Lloyd Toney. To be fair to Miss Shepardson, I have no doubt she had my best interests at heart, and her evaluations were appropriate, accurate, and given as exhortations to try harder. Memories are influenced by youthful interpretations, for sure, but maturity adds a more gracious reflection. In hindsight, I do believe she was a good teacher.

The hopeful rest of the story came about in 1970, following graduation from Bradley University. I was thankfully hired to teach a fourth-grade class at Homewood Heights Elementary School in Creve Coeur, next to East Peoria. A mutual admiration society blossomed between my delightful students and myself, and it was a very special year for all of us in many ways. The uniqueness of our activities contributed to the fun. Teaching them how to crochet was perhaps the most unusual project, but it's doubtful this could be done today. In that era, education was embracing a more wholistic approach, and learning this skill seemed a creative endeavor. Plus, it kept them busy when they had completed their work. They crocheted scarves and granny squares and were proud of their accomplishments. Me, too.

However, the academic curriculum was the most important, of course, and it included teaching my students how to solve word problems. I was determined to figure out the "mystery," and when I did, it was quite satisfying. The answer was setting up a proportional, fractional relationship with the given numbers. The simple application of a mathematics principle to create an understanding between the numbers and using their fraction location to tell me how to find the missing number through either multiplication or division changed everything, and it was a concept I was happy to teach. I think Miss Shepardson would have been proud of me!

The following August, Arie and I moved to Rhinelander, Wisconsin, where our son was born a year later. The students and I corresponded for a time, their letters still a joy to read. They shared information about their fifth-grade classes and the friendships I would remember. Jean D. sent her pretty school picture and wrote, *How are you? I miss you very much. Everybody talks about you.* Dalla C., who also sent a lovely photograph, ended one of her sweet notes with a tiny-print message, *any child who gets you as a mom is lucky.* Many of my letters are from another memorable student, Winston Ragon, who once delightfully wrote and misspelled his return address, *Gess Who!!!* His numerous letters express his kind and tenderhearted thoughts and bring a chuckle when observing how his salutations began with *Dear Mrs. Greenleaf* and became *Dear Ann* as time went by.

Letter ~ Winston Ragon, 1972

June 20, 1972

Dear Ann,

Hi, how are you and the expectant little one doing? (OK I hope.) How's your husband doing? How's summer in Wisconsin? If it's any cooler up there than it is down here I'll move up there. Now that school's out there's nothing to do, but that's what I do best, nothing. It's nearly 1:30 A.M. now but I'm not sleepy. You know, it's a funny thing but I've gone through 6 teachers including you and my kindergarten teacher but you're still the best. Well, I'm starting to get sleepy so good-bye. By the way I passed.
LOVE,
Winston Ragon
P.S.
The outside says return in 5 days but you don't have to, you don't even have to write back, I just hope you will.

Winston's sweet and thoughtful letter is shared as a "Thank you" to my teachers, the ones I didn't understand but grew to appreciate, and to those who demonstrated how a constructive teacher-student relationship makes a difference and contributes to the joy of living. I still have the letter from my eighth-grade English and Social Studies teacher, Mrs. Lois Spano (1924–2002), who wrote a thank-you note for the necklace-set I gave her. The faded envelope says *Miss Ann Brubaker (Andrew)*, a play on the combination of my first name and the first syllable of my last name, indicating the enjoyable, respectful nature of our relationship. An excerpt from her June 5, 1962, letter demonstrates her gracious spirit:

If I have been able to help you in any way, then my cup runneth over... I don't know what you will do with your life, but whatever it is, I think it will be successful. You have the gift of appreciating situations, people, and things. Don't lose that enthusiasm when you go into 9th grade. Don't be ashamed to be yourself, even though others are all conforming and acting in a stereotyped way ... Thanks again for the lovely remembrance. I hope the necklace and earrings last forever so that when I'm 79 I'll still be wearing them and remembering a very sweet girl who gave them to me.

We look ahead in life, never imagining we can't experience our expectations. Lois D. Spano sadly died from cancer ten months shy of her seventy-ninth birthday. She was thirty-eight when she wrote her message. I'm thankful for her impact and for the role model she presented not only as a teacher but as a wonderful human being. Gentle humor, positivity, and encouragement are unforgettable attributes and are impossible not to pass on. Her touch on my life was carried forward, and it's gratifying to know I had a small impact on Winston's life when he was in fourth grade. He entered law enforcement and became a valuable and successful deputy sheriff in his Illinois hometown and then in Knox County, Tennessee, where he retired. It has been a blessing to reconnect with him after all these years.

Chapter 14

Good Friends

My Connection to Mary Bewig Vermillon and "Steph Dilly,"
Daughter of Phyllis Diller
These yearbook messages convey the fun of those mid-teenage years,
when being *good friends* means everything.

SOME OF THE FRIENDSHIPS made in elementary school and carried into junior and senior high are still enjoyed today. It's especially meaningful that within my mountain community lives a friend I've known since second grade, Mary Bewig Vermillon. We have a lovely brunch together once a month, made even more special when her stylish and delightful older sister, Barb, comes for a visit and joins us. As young girls, Mary and I shared sleep overs, Girl Scouts, and train trips. Her ninth- and tenth-grade yearbook messages (1963,1964) convey the fun we had:

> You are really sweet and whatever we do it always turns out to be a PANIC!
> Love & hiccups! Mary.
> We've done a lot of talking on your front porch and all! [Our front porch swing was the place where conversations were shared, songs sung, books read, and dreams dreamed.] We have lots of fun memories!! Remember: The 'Lift' in Cincie, Coney Island, the train trips (playing BABY), Betty and the red lantern, the burglars,

shopping, Mike (?) Rickey (hum-m-m) JIM (ugh!) horses, and so much, much more. Oh, yes! Remember that day we decided we were gonna make some money? We did—about $1.00! Good luck always.

Love, Mary

Nothing has changed! As women blessed to be in our mid-seventies, we still love talking about everything. We share our faith, her remarkable oil paintings, and my writing endeavors. We take road trips to class reunions and encourage each other when life presents challenges. We marvel that we live in the same town after all these years, and our conversations usually include a warm reminiscence about the "good old days" of our childhood, especially since our friendship was enhanced through visits to Cincinnati, Ohio.

The summer after sixth grade, Mary and I were invited to visit our friend, Marcia G., who was moving to Cincinnati. Her original invitation was penned on a postcard showing three adorable collie puppies, still part of my postcard collection. We were to travel by train, leaving St. Louis Union Station to arrive at Cincinnati Union Terminal to stay a week with Marcia and her family. She wrote:

> Invited to come with Mary and you'd like it. We haven't set the date yet but I'll write and give you some dates and you can choose from them. You probably stay a week and then I'll come home with you on the train and stay here a week. I sure hope you can come. Love, Marcia

Mary and I made this trip three times, with our good friend Susie Knight Mayfield joining us for the second and perhaps third year, when Marica and her family lived in beautiful Mariemont, a Cincinnati suburb. Betty B., two years older in the Class of '64, came along once to visit Marcia's older brother, John, which added some impressionable romantic excitement.

Several weeks before each departure, Mom and I would drive to Union Station to purchase my ticket. Opening in 1894, the St. Louis Union Station was the largest in the world, and its awesome grandeur added to the thrill of the over 300-mile train ride across Illinois and Indiana to Ohio. This was the era when commercial travel meant dressing up, and for one of the trips, an elegant linen was chosen for a special outfit my mother sewed for the journey. It was a lovely pale green, and I was proud to wear it, but I still remember the wrinkles!

JUNE

Mom was always faithful to send a letter or postcard when I was away, and two postcard keepers were sent to Mariemont in 1961, one to my friends and one to me. My postcard is a picture of Union Station with news about home, and the other is a picture of two precious white kittens. Aware of the great time we were having, plus the extra work Marcia's mother would incur, Mom wrote, *Hello Girls—How was Coney?... Are you helping Jody—I hope. Have a nice trip home. We will see you Mon. Love to all —Mrs. B.*

Visiting Coney Island was always the highlight of our week in Cincinnati. All the rides were fun, but the Shooting Star roller coaster became a favorite. I rode it seven times in a row one summer, and Mary shared, "I totally remember going time and time again until our tickets ran out." Another special memory of Coney Island is from our third trip in 1962 when famous comedian Phyllis Diller (1917–2012) came out of the theater where she was performing to see Mary, primarily, who had spent the night with her daughter, Stephanie, a new friend from school.

In Diller's 2005 autobiography, *Like a Lampshade in a Whorehouse*, Phyllis describes her hectic work schedule and her desire for a quiet and settled environment to raise her family of five children (a son died in infancy). Since her husband, Sherwood Diller (1913–1993), had family living in the Webster Groves area, our community represented home. In the spring of 1962, Phyllis bought a Colonial-style, eleven-room house on Mason Avenue in Webster Park, painted an eye-catching soft pink. The Holy Redeemer Catholic Church and School complex on East Lockwood Avenue is still the corner neighbor to this house.

Phyllis's daughter Stephanie (1948–2002) was both beautiful and endearing with her long, thick auburn hair and appealing, fun-loving personality. I got to know her well, and she autographed my high school yearbooks (1963, 1964) with short but special messages, signing each *Steph Dilly*, to connect and yet distinguish herself from her famous mother. At the end of ninth grade she wrote, *We've been good friends this year—but just wait until next year. LOVE, Me (Steph Dilly)*, and drew a picture of herself with a big smile and her long hair flipped up on the ends, a common style. Stephanie always added a picture when she wrote a message, and in my tenth-grade yearbook a flower accompanied her comment about my becoming Junior Class secretary, *Hi Ann, Good Luck next year—you will be great—because you are. —Love, Steph (Dilly)*.

Over the three years the Diller family resided in Webster Groves, I received numerous invitations for sleepovers at her home and was introduced to Phyllis once when our paths crossed in the main foyer. She was low-key and gracious in meeting her daughter's friend, and I was thrilled for the personal introduction. Stephanie and I spent most of our time in her bedroom listening to records, a popular pastime, her favorite song, "I Left my Heart in San Francisco" by Tony Bennett played repeatedly. The longing for California, her home state, was very evident. The cook always prepared our breakfast, a glamorous notion, and the perfection of her tender, flaky biscuits has never been forgotten, nor matched.

My final memory about Stephanie is from my 1964 "Sweet Sixteen" birthday party at a local restaurant, a wonderful grown-up luncheon planned by my mother. Stephanie, who was born several weeks before me in the same month and year, brought a gift cleverly wrapped in fabric, a deep blue and green paisley print. The gift itself is long forgotten, but I still have the material folded away in a memory box. The uniqueness of receiving a gift so beautifully presented caught my imagination, and this unusual, out-of-the-ordinary occurrence indicated life doesn't always have to be wrapped in paper, a lesson I've never forgotten.

Phyllis moved her family back to California in 1965 when her marriage to Sherwood ended. I lost touch with my friend, but an online photograph shows Stephanie at age thirty-eight with her mother and sister and reveals a delightful woman. She married Marvin Earl Waldron (1922–2008) in 1973 and, according to some records, had one son. Stephanie tragically died from a stroke on July 4, 2002, at age fifty-three, way too young.

Junior and senior high school yearbook messages are a permanent record of the treasured and casual friendships and the fun experienced in those transitional teenage years. Each comment conveys life as it was lived in that era and is forever part of our personal, American story.

Chapter 15

The President Kennedy Era

My Connection to Gail Monroe Crosson and the Peace Corps
This reminiscence shares the *goodwill* fostered by the Peace Corps and expresses the *incredible gift* this organization gives to all involved.

AT THE END OF sixth grade (1959–1960), several months before the start of Junior High, my dear friend Susie Knight Mayfield hosted a "Beatnik Party," which made a distinct cultural memory. I had spent many delightful sleepovers at Susie's lovely home in Webster Park, with its unique architectural design and setting. Her mother, Nan, was an excellent artist who guided many of our Girl Scout troop art projects. She worked with Audree McConnell, our outstanding Girl Scout leader who led our troop for seven remarkable years and was the mother of our good friend, Tina. The party took place downstairs near Nan's studio, where the area was transformed with a décor and vibe centered on the "beatnik era." This meant low lights and beaded streamers, much like the coffee houses that drew "Beatniks" who read their poetry or played their music before an appreciative audience.

Several years after the end of World War II, Jack Kerouac (1922–1969), an American novelist and poet, labeled himself and his like-minded contemporaries, e.g., Allen Ginsberg and William S. Burroughs, the "Beat Generation," individuals who were committed to rejecting mainstream norms to embrace artistic freedom through jazz music, pensive poetry, and contemplative literature. Adherents wore distinctive black clothing and berets and lived a very soulful and intriguing life. Herb Caen, a columnist for the *San Francisco Chronicle*, coined the term "Beatnik" in 1958, a label meant to be demeaning, but instead it became a comprehensively acceptable word. We relished the idea of taking on a Beatnik persona for the party, dressed accordingly, and enjoyed the evening immensely. One unforgettable game had two teams passing a grapefruit from chin to chin, boy to girl. If it was dropped, the team had to start over. The proximity to people of interest (namely, being next to the boy one had a crush on, or vice versa) was exciting and made the experience especially memorable for those of us on the brink of leaving elementary school for junior high.

The second distinct cultural memory, one that broadens to encompass a tragic historical event, centers on Gail Monroe Crosson, the older sister of my very dear high school friend, Linda Monroe Yust. Linda and I experienced a wide scope of teenage life together with much laughter and camaraderie. We were inspired when Gail made the decision to join the Peace Corps at age twenty-two, and her father agreed. *My dad, Paul Monroe, who adored the Peace Corps, was all for her going!* wrote Linda. She added, *My mom, Lucille, was very much against her going because of both her age and the fact she still had a ½ year of college to complete. So, some difference of opinion there!* (Very understandable.) Gail had finished three and a half years at the University of Ohio, but she was a child of the 1960s and was determined to live accordingly. She left for Brazil in February 1965 and returned home in June of 1967 after a life-changing, almost two and a half years of service in South America. Once she was home, she completed her final semester at "Mizzou," the University of Missouri, much to her mother's relief. Gail graciously shared some of her fascinating Peace Corps memories and observations (2025). Her experience had its squeamish moments, but her relationship with the people is inspirational!

This humanitarian government agency was established by President John F. Kennedy on March 1, 1961. He chose his brother-in-law, Sargent Shriver, to direct and advance his vision to aid developing countries using the skills and talents of idealistic individuals, like Gail, willing to volunteer and assist in the areas of education, agriculture, health, and community development. According to the current Peace Corps website, *Since its inception, over 200,000 volunteers have served in 139 countries.* An additional note-worthy statistic states, *In 1966, over 15,000 volunteers were working in the field.* I'm not surprised. The youth of this era wanted to make a difference in the world by helping others, inspired by the role models around them. When the Peace Corps started, it offered another avenue for service, a romantic and appealing opportunity born out of the inspiration of a charismatic President who was tragically assassinated before our eyes in Dallas, Texas, on Friday, November 22, 1963.

I saw President Kennedy in person, at a distance, twice in one day. His campaign for the presidency brought him to our area in the early fall of 1960, and he spoke outdoors at the Crestwood Shopping Center Plaza near our community. His uplifting speech, personality, and charm made him a favorite. Later in the day, I was in Old Orchard, a small, quaint shopping district in Webster Groves, and Kennedy drove by in an open-air convertible. Sixty-five years later, it was thrilling when Linda confirmed my sighting. *Our dad also saw him in the convertible that day! He was very proud of that moment, Kennedy being his favorite president. We lived on South Old Orchard, just about a mile away.* The joyful memory of that day makes the tragedy of his assassination and its aftermath even more heart wrenching. When something of great magnitude occurs, we usually remember "where we were" when we either learned or experienced it, and in my case, President Kennedy's death was announced at the end of a Student Council meeting in tenth grade.

We were glued to the television set all weekend, trying to glean any piece of news. On Sunday morning, those who were home and watching were incredulous to witness, live, Jack Ruby shoot and kill the alleged assassin, Lee Harvey Oswald, as Oswald was being transported through the basement of the Dallas Police Headquarters. It seemed all of life was out of control! I stayed home from school on Monday to watch the riveting funeral service from beginning to end, joining millions to view the enormity of this tragic and historic day. As the grand solemnity unfolded, my feelings ran the gamut from a broken heart to awe. Mesmerized by the family, I couldn't turn away from the dignified grace and beauty of our widowed First Lady, Jacqueline Bouvier Kennedy (1929–1994), and the devastating innocence of their children, Caroline age five and John Jr. age two, as they each said their "good-byes" to their husband and father.

President Kennedy's assassination changed the course of America in profound ways, ushering in the growth of a despicable mindset that chooses death as an unconscionable way to express grievances and disagreements. America saw this occur again, twice within the next five years when Martin Luther King Jr. (1929–1968) was assassinated on April 4, 1968, in Memphis,

Tennessee, and Robert F. Kennedy (1925–1968) was shot two months later, June 5, 1968, in Los Angeles, California, dying the next day. Sorrow upon sorrow upon sorrow rocked our country.

This occurred while our nation was also dealing with the Vietnam War, a quagmire which reached its peak in that out-of-control year, 1968. American troop levels were at a staggering 540,000 service men, and 300 American soldiers were dying each week from the fighting (Zunes and Laird, Jan. 2010). The "US Anti-Vietnam War Movement" (1964–1973) escalated at this point, having started in 1964 when the United States first bombed North Vietnam and troops were sent in the following year. The official movement ended in January 1973 when Henry Kissinger, Secretary of State to President Nixon, brokered the Paris Peace Accords, the troops were withdrawn, and the draft was suspended, creating an all-volunteer military.

Through it all, somehow, life continued. Grief was tempered, happiness experienced, and while we would never forget the despair we felt in this decade, it was clear that embracing the joy and hope available every new day was our only way forward.

> *Cause me to hear Your lovingkindness in the morning,*
> *For in You do I trust;*
> *Cause me to know the way in which I should walk,*
> *For I lift up my soul to You.*
> (Psalm 143:8 NJKV)

A Peace Corps Reminiscence ~ Gail Monroe Crosson, 2025

I WAS A VOLUNTEER in Brazil in the early days of the Peace Corps. We had intensive training for 3 months stateside at a university . . . in my case, it was the University of Arizona. Half of our group was deselected for various reasons and the rest of us were flown to Rio and then spread out in sites across the country. I was first in a town called Garanhuns and lived with a pediatric nurse. I gave shots and volunteered in an orphanage. My site mate delivered babies but really, our biggest job was PR, I think. We weren't necessarily trained for specific jobs like the volunteers of today. It was the Kennedy days and people loved Americans. They loved us in spite of our lack of skills. (I was a fine arts major.)

My next town was Tracunhaem which translated to "the feeding pan of the ants." It was tiny, poor, rural and most of the people had no education. My house had no running water, intermittent electricity, sticks holding up tiles for a roof, dirt floor, hammocks for sleeping, and an outhouse with no door and no ceiling. HUGE insects and reptiles!!!

The dominant activity in town was production of utilitarian pottery. The potters made large pots which held water for both washing and drinking. The women filled small pots with water from a pond. They carried these pots on their heads and then poured the water into the larger pots in their homes. There were always tadpoles swimming in our jugs, and we had to remove them on a regular basis. The water, of course, was not safe to drink and had to be boiled before we could use it. Very primitive methods.

There were a few people creating folk art and that was my main focus, trying to produce and export their craft. Today, the town has water and electricity and has become a folk-art destination in NE Brazil. This was not because of me but rather a gradual, natural evolution. I was just there at the beginning.

As I said, Peace Corps in those early days was so much goodwill. I can honestly say that the experience of living in another country, learning their culture, their language and forming close relationships was a highlight in my life. The people were poor, gracious, joyous and willingly shared whatever they had. There were no phones, no TV, no newspapers, just long evenings of talking, singing and playing music. An incredible gift for which I am ever grateful!

Chapter 16

Television Tells a Story

My Connection to Sixteen in Webster Groves
Our tenth- and twentieth-year Reunion Booklets, 1976 and 1986, compiled experiences, achievements, and answers about the first reality shock after high school, and about what we remember from those teenage years.

HIGH SCHOOL REUNIONS ELICIT a variety of responses, ranging from a verbal, "You haven't changed a bit" to a private reflection on how life changes all of us, one way or another. We observe, smile, and wonder together about the passage of time. We interact happily with old friends, share our mutual memories, and chat enthusiastically with others we knew in high school, though perhaps not well. Reunions showcase our "rest of the story" successes but hidden beneath our well-calculated appearances lie all the conundrums and challenges of life. Certainly, for each person, the pendulum has swung between happiness and grief.

Our ten-year reunion committee was coordinated by Patricia Corrigan Krauska. She was the perfect choice. When we met in Mrs. Alderman's seventh grade homeroom class at Plymouth Junior High School, Pat became a very close *B.F.Y.* (Best Friend You), as stated in every yearbook message. At the end of twelfth grade she wrote, *We've been together six years, and we've been friends since I saw "ANN" written on your notebook.* Through all the joys and sorrows shared, writing was a common thread.

Pat achieved an outstanding literary career, publishing hundreds of articles and over thirty books, ranging from nature and animal themes to inspire children of all ages, to the sights and delights of San Francisco for adults. She initially wrote for *The St. Louis Globe-Democrat* before it closed, starting her successful twenty-three-year career at the *St. Louis Post-Dispatch* in 1982. She worked, *as a news reporter, food writer, restaurant critic, theater critic, night city editor, feature columnist, travel writer, health and fitness writer, and fashion writer* (PATRICIA CORRIGAN PAPERS, State Historical Society of Missouri Research Center). Pat was chosen for the Webster Groves High School (WGHS) Wall of Fame in 1989, established to recognize graduates who have meaningfully contributed to their field of work or philanthropy. The whole of her remarkable career was still in the future when she led the reunion committee.

Working with a group of close friends, Pat helped organize a memorable weekend, and along with her committee compiled a fascinating publication, *The Spirit of '66, Webster Groves High School Tenth Reunion 1976*. The booklet was a treasure to receive and remains a deeply meaningful presentation of achievements and thoughts about life. At the time, receiving it in the mail soothed the disappointment for those of us not attending the reunion. My good friend, Carol Shankland Porter, who was on the committee, had married in the intervening years and wrote the Foreword, signing her reflection, Carol S. Kennedy:

> We were seniors, ready to go out and make the big time ... the whole Breathless on the Threshold of Life routine. For many of us, the betrayal of "Sixteen in Webster Groves" provided the only inkling of what unpleasantries the real world might hold in store. So from a personal perspective, the spirit of '66 was naive, trusting and hopeful. That spring, The Lovin' Spoonful filled the air with daydreams. Who could ask for a better year to take on the world than the year 1966?

In our final year of high school, a nine-member CBS film crew spent the entire month of November 1965 following the lives of high school juniors to ultimately amass twenty-two hours of film documenting their thoughts, activities, and realities (Start, *Webster Groves*, 233). Seniors were also interviewed, as well as parents and assorted others. The television documentary was titled *Sixteen in Webster Groves*. Later, Charles Kuralt

(1934–1997), the program narrator, said they were looking to uncover "youthful rebellion and dissatisfaction" (Conklin, "56 in Webster Groves," 2006). Would they find rebellion in beautiful, stately Webster Groves, a middle- to upper-middle-class St. Louis suburb with century-old homes and sheltering trees nestled within the heartland of America? Did anyone in Webster *know* this was their intent, a documentary portraying teenage angsts and anger?

Most people were thrilled to learn there would be a television program about high school students in our beloved community. Surely, the gracious attributes, faith, and traditions we cherished (and no doubt took for granted) would be emphasized. We had pride in our town and were grateful to live here, so naturally the storyline would embrace these positives. The program, certainly, would also make clear that academic achievement was important, even valued. We were raised to be students who would pursue education beyond high school by attending, of course, college, but other options included career and trade schools where, e.g., secretarial skills and automotive training provided good future employment. Nursing degree programs were offered at several St. Louis hospitals, providing an alternative to a four-year college degree. Of course, wanting to go to college or a similar discipline would be portrayed positively and worth the effort it took to get there. But, as it turned out, how wrong we were!

As a rule, parents hope their children will surpass them in achievement, and our parents were no different. In my family, Mom had a college degree and Dad didn't, and no doubt a percentage of Webster parents had a similar composition, or neither parent had a degree. Our parents were the Greatest Generation, and the enormity of their circumstances influenced what they could personally achieve and what they wanted for their children. We understood and would heed the call, but since we were raised to be independent, we would ultimately do it our way. We had our own thoughts about success, believing it encompassed more than material gain. But our Baby Boomer Generation didn't face The Great Depression or World Wars I and II, so we had the luxury of thinking, perhaps, more altruistically. Our parents were definitely caring, but their focus was certainly career oriented.

In the documentary, some parents are presented in a very poor, even embarrassing light. It appears their sole interest is in their child's future earning success. Nothing in the program explains why these parents felt as they did, nor did the interviews encompass a wide socioeconomic group. Our innocent desire to emulate or maybe surpass and broaden what our parents achieved turns out to be incredulous to the producers. "Youthful rebellion and dissatisfaction," where is it? We were teenagers, so it existed, but we were pragmatic. Afterall, we were from the Midwest, steadfast and knee deep in practicality.

Interestingly, eight years prior in 1958, a Webster Groves family was chosen to be featured in an NBC documentary for *Wide Wide World* (1955–1958), the Sunday afternoon television series narrated by Dave Garroway (1913–1982). He was the founding anchor of *Today*, hosting this new NBC morning show for nine years (1952–1961), a program usually playing in the background as we got ready for school. The family chosen for the 1958 episode titled "The House in Webster Groves" wasn't just any family, it was the Carl and Margaret Hay Bewig family. It was my fourth-grade classmate's family, my dear friend Mary Bewig Vermillon.

Mary and her parents; her older brother and sister, Carl and Barbara; and their grandmother, Mary Hay, who lived with them, were chosen because their family configuration and demographics matched the *statistical picture* drawn by economists in the Department of Commerce. Ted Rogers, the producer, identified the Bewigs as "the typical American family . . . owning their own home in the suburbs but struggling a bit to make ends meet" (Start, "Bewigs of Webster Groves," 1958).

Clarissa Start Lippert (1917–2008), a reporter for the *St. Louis Post-Dispatch* for thirty-four years until retirement, plus an additional thirty years as a monthly columnist, lived in our community. Her comprehensive article about this television program is titled, "Bewigs of Webster Groves to be Featured Today on Wide Wide World Show." Published on February 16, 1958, Start's interview with Mrs. Bewig demonstrates how the Greatest Generation believed in higher education for their children, a notion later expressed by the students and parents in *Sixteen in Webster Groves*. She mentions they had visited colleges to determine the best one for Carl, and she made a comparative statement about the realities of her generation:

> The program will begin with high school students and their dreams of a rosy future. This doesn't exactly apply to us because we went through that period of our lives during the depression and we didn't dream of great wealth or fame, just of having enough to live on.

I spent a thoughtful hour watching my high school documentary again, knowing that sociology classes view the program to learn about life in the mid-1960s. How strange it must appear and totally unrelatable, for that was my reaction to most of it, and I was there! Sixty years later, the interviews, scenes, and setup seem even more stilted, contrived, and exclusionary than remembered. When the filming didn't go as expected, Kuralt is clearly surprised with the conformity of thought about education and future success. The community was surprised, too, by the distortions presented. Immediate viewer response ranged from hostility to agreement, and from inaccurate to accurate. It is understood that journalism works within a space or time allotment and expresses a theme or agenda. However, what was left out in the documentary made the program especially troubling.

Clarissa Start was commissioned by the city council to write the history of our community in honor of America's Bicentennial, and her book, *Webster Groves* (1975), contains a relevant chapter, "Sixteen in—Where?" She succinctly describes the contrivance of the program, the trust families had in opening their homes to the producers, and the betrayal and hurt individuals felt when the film was edited to portray not only them but their children in such a negative and lopsided light.

The initially scheduled release for the television program had been postponed, but on February 25, 1966, the night finally arrived. Community excitement and anticipation led to numerous "Watch Parties" planned for the big event, and several friends came over to my house to see the program. The somber opening scene identified the students as "children of privilege, of affluence" and established the tone and intent of the program. As the documentary unfolded, our initial excitement turned to increasing dismay and disbelief. Our cherished community ended up being portrayed as superficial, insular, shallow, and an indifferent enclave of privileged families and students, with dreams centered solely on financial success and achievement. We were stunned.

Pat Corrigan, who was a budding journalist even then, was at our home that night as a liaison reporter for the *St. Louis Globe Democrat*. Soon after the program ended, Pat called the newspaper, and we were both interviewed over the telephone for our immediate thoughts. Our comments were published the next day, February 26, 1966, in an article titled "Webster Groves Upset by TV Show." My mother saved two newspaper clippings from the *Globe Democrat* concerning reactions to the documentary. They are now dis-colored, gently frayed and fragile. One article includes our telephone quotes, and the other is Pat's extensive article which came out a week later. My response then is still my response:

... Seventeen-year-old Ann Brubaker, however, was angry that the students had been accused of lacking imagination.

"We do have imagination, we do think, we do worry about the problems of the world," she said. "The man who said that didn't know what he was talking about."

The students' world is a status-conscious one, said the program.

"The students care very little about class and social status," said Ann. "They care because the parents care. It's the parents who push them and see they go to the right parties . . . I wish they had shown some more representative parents."

Support for this came from Robert Chapman, past president of the Webster Groves Chamber of Commerce, who said: "I certainly don't agree with some of the low opinions expressed by the parents about the sixteen-year-olds. I give them (the teenagers) credit for knowing a lot."

. . . Said 17-year-old Webster Groves High School student Patricia Corrigan: "I'm all shook up. The students are trying to please their parents, but this program tonight gave me a bad view of some of the parents in Webster Groves."

. . . Said the narrator of the hour-long program "To be 16 in Webster Groves is to be insulated, but it is possible to see the dim world of the outside occasionally . . . Theirs is not a world of rebellion, dissatisfaction and adventure,"

. . . Dr. Arthur C. Barron, CBS producer of the program, said here afterwards, "We had many calls at Kmox-Tv after the program. They divided into two classes. The ones who called in to say they agreed and the ones who were mad as a hornet's nest."

This article was followed by Pat's full-length feature story in the *St. Louis Globe Democrat* published March 4, 1966, titled "Webster Groves: Are Teens Still Clad in Diapers?" Her story shares interviews and observations about what was missing in the documentary, omissions which defined my life and the life of my friends. Pat presents final, insightful thoughts about the whole experience. Steve Swigert, my friend and fellow actor who played my secret husband, his Tony to my Marge, in our high school production of *Out of the Frying Pan*, stated an underlying, inherently applicable truth, "It is impossible to give a true picture of any town in one hour," he said. "With that in mind, CBS accomplished its purpose fairly well. Parts were slightly overdone, but just to make it entertaining television material."

Reunion Booklets, 1976 and 1986

THE SPIRIT OF '66 AND *WG 66 CLASS REUNION 86*

The memories, achievements, and hopes compiled for both the tenth- and twentieth-year anniversary booklets offered a thoughtful summation of experiences after high school. In *The Spirit of '66*, Patricia Corrigan Krauska, General Coordinator of the 1976 reunion summarizes the unforgettable impact of *Sixteen in Webster Groves*:

> *Marcia Westphalen Pattillo* and *Judy Willis Wenzel* [my italics] reported they were amazed to discover that "Sixteen in Webster Groves" was telling it like it was. As *Judy* put it, "We were really as sheltered as the tv special portrayed us to be." Ten other graduates also mentioned a change of perspective once out of high school which illustrated to them just how sheltered our lives were, nestled away in the confines of 100 Selma Ave. and thereabouts.

My intent was to share numerous comments from the reunion booklets, for they were all meaningful. However, how does one pick and choose? Inevitably, someone would be left out who should have been included. Instead, three relevant thoughts from the heart conclude this chapter:

REALITY SHOCK (1976); SYNOPSIS and I REMEMBER (1986)

Ann Brubaker Greenleaf: [I Remember, 1986] We visited St. Louis in March; drove by the home, the church, the schools (how could they tear Plymouth down? I always wanted to go back and visit my teachers!), the library, the Y, through Old Orchard and Webster, even by the Cemetery dear Dad. These places of my life—of my heart—that mean nothing to my patient family but everything to this person who was influenced by and who reflects those special years when to be 8 or 12 or even 16 in Webster Groves was to be the luckiest person alive.

Robert Morgan: [Synopsis, 1986] Ten years ago my highest priority was making myself happy. A co-worker began talking to me about the Bible . . . I asked hard questions . . . He answered and showed me I had sinned . . . God made me righteous in His sight, not worthy by myself, but through Christ I am acceptable to God. My life is changed and my priorities are now in the right order: God first . . . me last. No, I don't always live that way, but with God's help I try.

Carol Shankland Kennedy: [Reality Shock, 1976] Not the first, but one of the most significant: compiling an in memoriam list for this book.

> IN MEMORIAM
> I've seen fire and I've seen rain.
> I've seen sunny days that I thought
> would never end.
> I've seen lonely times when I could not
> find a friend.
> But I always thought that I'd see you again . . .
> (James Taylor, "Fire and Rain," 1970)

Chapter 17

Too Soon an Ending

My Connection to Carol Shankland Kennedy Porter
This letter from my dear high school friend, Carol Shankland
Kennedy Porter, was written ten years after our high school graduation
in response to my condolences for the tragic and untimely death
of Charles G., whom she dated throughout high school.
Her touching letter is relatable in every area, especially in loss,
at times, I find I am still dealing with it.

GRADUATION FROM HIGH SCHOOL launches everyone into realities that are but a shadow in our student years. Love, hurt, success, failure, acquisition, loss, war, peace, life, and death will all unfold over the span of each lifetime. But on graduation night, the future is still, usually, an idealistic, rosy unknown. As it turned out, 1966 was a benchmark year. Our graduating class was the last to simply assume and accept the norms and behaviors of what had been a traditional, 1950s-oriented society. Things were already starting to change with the Civil and Women's Rights Movements making inroads into American's conscience, but the Vietnam War (1961–973) upended everything.

As shared, Carol wrote the Foreword for *The Spirit of '66, Webster Groves High School Tenth Reunion 1976* and began with a description of the innocence of our graduating class. She then addresses the social revolution that took place primarily in response to the war's escalation. This new era was soon identified as "The Age of Aquarius," the name taken from the opening song in the hit Broadway musical *Hair* (1967), titled "Aquarius/Let the Sunshine In" (lyrics: James Rado and Gerome Ragni; music: Galt MacDermot; album: The 5th Dimension, 1969). The song's utopian lyrics and haunting melody spoke dramatically to our culture's desire for attitudinal and behavioral changes, achieved through a renouncement of traditional values. Carol writes:

> We were urged to tune in, turn on, drop out, to the accompaniment of strobe lights and acid rock . . . Some of the madness was personal. By 1969 we were wearing skirts up to our navels and singing "Why Don't We Do It In The Road?" This after a heritage of Teen Town parties where chaperones busted couples for dancing double-clutch. This just three short years after sweet sixteen corsages, the wet look and white socks were still socially acceptable.

We didn't know it was the end of an era when we walked the aisle on graduation night in June 1966, but it was. Soon after, some of our classmates went directly into military service, but most went to college, some to take advantage of the exemptions offered in selected fields of study. However, with voluntary army recruitment dropping off in opposition to the war, the draft lottery system was implemented on December 1, 1969, targeting men born between 1944 and 1950. The government was attempting to broaden the socio-economic and racial makeup of the military, as well as to increase the availability of men needed to fight in Southeast Asia.

As the death toll for our soldiers mounted, so did outright repulsion for the war. Draft cards were burned, people who refused to serve were imprisoned, and many fled to Canada to avoid being drafted into the military. Our soldiers came home to disheartening jeers instead of appreciation, so they discretely made a return to civilian life and rarely spoke about their time in the war. Some experienced PTSD (Post-Traumatic Stress Disorder). Two parallel universes existed, one for returning veterans, and one for everyone else.

The Vietnam Conflict Extract Data File of DCAS (Defense Casualty Analysis System) tells the story of lives ending way too soon for the American men and women who served, and of the scope of grief they left behind. According to its website, *DCAS Extract Files contains records of 58,220 U.S. military fatal casualties of the Vietnam War*. The following is a statistical bell curve of loss and despair for a cause that seemed, perhaps, reasonable at first, the U.S. policy to contain communism and protect South Vietnam and the region from its insurgence. When mounting casualties made achieving this goal too high a cost, rebellion occurred against basically *everything*.

> DCAS Vietnam Conflict Extract File record counts by INCIDENT OR DEATH DATE (Year) (as of April 29, 2008):
> Year of Death—Number of Records:
> 1962—53; 1963—122
> 1964—216; 1965—1,928
> 1966—6,350; 1967—11,363
> 1968—16,899; 1969—11,780
> 1970—6,173; 1971—2,414
> 1972—759; 1973—68

As the war unfolded, the Beatniks of the Beat Generation morphed into the Hippies of the Hippie Movement which espoused similar, anti-establishment viewpoints and took them to the point of a total rejection of societal norms. Opposition to the Vietnam War was huge in the movement's growth, where "make love not war" became the defining expression, and free love was encouraged among adherents, derisively called "flower children" by some. The drugs LSD and marijuana lent their influence, and the music of some of my favorite artists, the group Peter, Paul and Mary; Joan Baez, The Beatles, and Bob Dylan came to define the "hippie culture." I never got deeply involved in the movement, per se, but the war's futility became clear and the terrible loss of life for all the countries involved made the war's end *imperative*. As it turned out, whether one embraced the whole of the Hippie Movement or not, our cultural appearance and daily choices were influenced by their trademark look. From rimless "granny glasses" to floor-length "granny dresses," from long hair to seeking a more natural, "back-to-the-earth," wholistic lifestyle, this counterculture movement fostered an ecological approach to living that is still appreciated and practiced.

In September 2019, just before the Covid pandemic shut down normal life throughout our country and the world, several from our church went to Washington, DC, as part of "The 400-Voice American Festival Choir." Organized by Celebration Concert Tours International, founded by current CEO and President Dr. Phil Barfoot, we sang at the Kennedy Center in a program called *Worship in Washington* featuring three well-known Christian singing artists, Sandi Patty, Travis Cottrell, and Taranda Greene. It was a memorable evening to top off a memorable visit to our nation's capital.

We spent several days viewing most of our treasured national monuments, including the Lincoln and Jefferson Memorials, powerful, breathtaking, and majestic. At the World War II Memorial, we talked with the late Senator Bob Dole (1923–2021) from Kansas, who was greeting visitors with a smile and a good wish as he sat in his wheelchair, a three-time decorated WWII hero with two Purple Hearts and a Bronze Star.

On our way to Arlington National Cemetery, we stopped to see the U.S. Marine Corps' stunning Iwo Jima Memorial located outside the cemetery. The design depicts the iconic February 23, 1945, photograph of six soldiers raising the American flag in victory on Mount Suribachi, located on Iwo Jima, one of the Japanese Volcano Islands. The picture taken by Associated Press photographer Joe Rosenthal riveted the nation and inspired this deeply moving memorial dedicated to *the Marine dead of all wars and their comrades of other services who fell fighting beside them.*

We witnessed the somber changing of the guard at the Tomb of the Unknown Soldier and visited the President John F. Kennedy Memorial, his Gravesite and the Eternal Flame sobering reminders of that unforgettable day, November 22, 1963, when tragedy befell our nation. Located southeast of the JFK Memorial is the gravesite for his brother, Robert F. Kennedy, invoking much thought about all this family has given and lost. Perhaps "solemn beauty" can describe the Washington, DC, monuments and locations. Certainly, the depth of loss, sorrow, and sacrifice in each instance is impossible to express or fathom.

Visiting these storied sites is emotional, but for those who lived through the turmoil of the times, it is especially moving to see the Dr. Martin Luther King Jr. and the Vietnam Veterans Memorials. The National Park Service website eloquently describes Dr. King's site, which was dedicated in 2011:

> King's memorial is the first to honor an African American individual on the National Mall. The space is a place to contemplate Martin Luther King, Jr.'s legacy: a non-violent philosophy striving for freedom, justice, and equality.
>
> In 2000, the judges selected ROMA Design Group's plan for a stone with Dr. King's image emerging from a mountain. The plan's theme referenced a line from King's 1963 "I Have a Dream" speech:
>
> "With this faith, we will be able to hew out of the mountain of despair a stone of hope."

The Vietnam Veterans Memorial also invokes contemplation. The powerful recognition of over 58,000 men and women who served and died during the Vietnam War is intense. The low-slung, shiny black granite, V-shaped monument stuns with its breathtaking, 200-foot simplicity. Every name of every person lost in the war is engraved on the wall next to the date of their fatal injury, the chronological order of this date determining the name's location. Tears accompany the search for family or friend, with an etching usually made to honor the loved one and commemorate the visit. Designed by architect Maya Lin and dedicated on Veteran's Day 1982, the U.S. Department of Defense describes the memorial's impact and other war-related monuments on the site:

> It's the most-visited memorial on the National Mall in Washington, attracting more than 5 million people each year . . . The memorial also features the Three Servicemen statue, the Vietnam Women's Memorial, the In Memory plaque, and a flagpole with an etching of the insignia of what were the country's five military branches.

Death always surprises, even when expected, regardless the age of the individual. To be alive and then not is startling. It is an earthly finality, with more to come. Still, even with the promise of eternal life, death leaves a void and longing heartache for the loved one(s) who have experienced "Too Soon an Ending."

> For God so loved the world that He gave His only begotten Son,
> that whoever believes in Him should not perish
> but have everlasting life.
> (John 3:16 NKJV)

Letter ~ Carol Shankland Kennedy, 1976

30 June 76

Dear Ann—
How nice to get such a thoughtful letter from you. I'm glad you liked the book [*The Spirit of 66, Webster Groves High School Tenth Reunion 1976*]—Susan [Charlesworth Ward], Linda [Monroe Yust] and I worked very hard on it, so it's always nice to get some appreciative feedback. I'll pass along your comments.

I hope you will excuse <u>this</u> paper—I was sitting down to draft some freelance stuff but in my usual procrastinating manner, thought it would be more fun to write a note to you. But I don't know how coherent this will be. In the past couple weeks, I have had a heady dose (overdose, actually) of those awesome life experiences you referred to in your letter.

First, the reunion. It was weird—I felt like I was in a time warp. I sorely missed several people who weren't there—especially Charles (more about him in a minute). I am never comfortable in a large gathering, and I think I just kind of put myself on "automatic." So basically the way I feel about the reunion is this: I wish somebody would write a review of the evening so I could read about what happened!

The following Thursday at work I bashed my head on the corner of a shelf. I had it x-rayed & there were no fractures or concussions, but the doctor said to take it easy. It <u>still</u> feels weird. (I learned soon after that I actually did have a concussion.)

The next day my grandmother died. It wasn't unexpected! She'd had terminal cancer, made even more difficult by serious injuries she sustained in a fall. She suffered a great deal and was ready to go . . . but none of the rest of us were really ready, even though we'd thought we were.

JUNE

The day after she died was Bruce G.'s wedding. I've kept in close contact with that family all these years and had felt honored that Steve [Carol's husband] and I were invited. I was going to cancel in light of my grandmother's death, but Mother thought we ought to go. So we did, and that was another weird excursion into the past. (Bruce looks very much like Charles.)

Sunday was spent at the funeral parlor & Monday was the funeral. I tried to go back to work yesterday but my head was foggy inside & throbbing on the outside. (I look like Cyclops)—hence I am home today and sounding very much like Mary Hartman, I fear.

I'll devote one more gloomy paragraph to Charles G. before moving on to happier subjects. For some reason I thought you knew . . . he was killed in a one-car accident in July 1970 as he was driving home from San Francisco on Navy leave. I wonder at it, too, Ann. Of all people. I mean, to think that a person like Charles dies while Alice Cooper lives on! That was very definitely "my first reality shock after leaving Webster Groves High School" and the most difficult thing I've ever had to deal with. At times, I find I am still dealing with it. (The In Memoriam page was my personal tribute to Charles, as well as to the other people listed there.) Steve (who never knew him, but in fact "babysat" with me during the year I spent getting through the aftermath of his death) and I have agreed that if we ever have a son, we'll name him Charles. [And they did.]

So that's the story on my current finished and unfinished business. The yearbook entry should fill you in on the rest of what I'm doing. Even though you could obviously tell by the Foreword that I'm—er—rather <u>ruminative</u>, I have been enjoying life and actually smile occasionally! From your letter I gather you're still a real contemplator and we could probably have a fine time getting together and analyzing things to a pulp. I'm glad life has treated you well, even though as you say, it <u>is</u> amazing to witness both the control and lack of control we have over it. Just as one hits her 20's and discovers she has the power to run her own life, some really heavy thing—like a death—comes along to reinstill a little humility!

Day after tomorrow we're leaving for Edina, MO, to spend July 4th weekend with Steve's parents. And when we come back . . . I will plunge into all the domestic & professional projects that have gone neglected for so long—first because of the reunion, now a bit longer because of the past week's happenings. (My most burning ambition right now is to get my woolens to the dry cleaner's before September!) Anyway, that's why

I'm writing you today, despite my hazy head—because after 4th weekend, I won't be doing any personal correspondence for a long time.

And I didn't want to put off thanking you for your good wishes. You must have a 6th sense where timing is concerned! Best wishes to you and Arie—and Arie Todd—let's not wait another 10 years to get back in touch?

Love,
Carol

JULY

CHAPTER 18 . . . A SOUTHERN HERITAGE

My Connection to Frances Webber Brubaker
American History: The Revolutionary War, Slavery, The Civil War

CHAPTER 19 . . . HEADING WEST

My Connection to Frances Webber Brubaker
Letter: Frances Webber Brubaker, 1967

Chapter 18

A Southern Heritage

My Connection to Frances Webber Brubaker
American History is our ancestors' lives lived out on the breathtaking stage of our beautiful continent, east to west, north to south.

HERITAGE. WE STAND IN awe. Every person has a family story. It is filled with events and aspects that astonish in the knowing and cause humility at the wonder of our being here. How did the complexities of each family history track generation after generation and now, here we are? How did our ancestors survive wars and famine, bondage and sickness, fear and loss? What was it like to cross the oceans of the world? What were the hopes? The whys? The cruelties? The joys?

The history shared in this chapter, and the next two, touches on what occurred in our nation's story to establish and profoundly shape and change our country. These events are found in most American genealogies, for our ancestors are known for their large families. Since siblings possess the same ancestry, each descending line takes family history both downward and outward, creating a vast connection of shared narratives. This book is simply the many narrowed down to one, an expression of the commonality of our American story and an encouragement for others to seek knowledge about their own family.

JULY

My Grandmother Frances "Fanny" Webber Brubaker (1878–1975) has deep American roots. Her heritage includes two southern states and communities with storied histories: Jamestown, Virginia; and Boonesborough, Kentucky. Slavery is part of the line, a sad but not surprising reality, and the push into Kentucky meant troublesome encounters with the Indians. Her ancestry traces back to England, with the Webber family leaving Somerset and arriving in Virginia before the late 1600s. Marriage would later unite them with the Goosey family of Lancashire, who arrived in the colony soon after. The Hill family from Devon came even earlier to the Virginia Colony, in the mid-1600s. They would join with the Combs family, the first to arrive, leaving *Combs Manor, in Devonshire, England, for Jamestown, Virginia, in 1619* (Miller, "Mayflower Docked Later," 1959). Individuals from these four families moved to Kentucky in the Daniel Boone era, settling in the neighboring Madison and Clark Counties. They traveled through the Cumberland Gap on the Wilderness Road, a buffalo and Indian trail enlarged by Boone and his men to make a viable route through the southern Appalachian Mountains. For the next thirty-five years, the lure of the unsettled, fertile land stretching beyond the Cumberland Mountains would bring over 300,000 people westward through the gap (history.com).

Kentucky and Daniel Boone (1734–1820) are synonymous. Boone *came in March 1775* (Chenault, "Brave Defenders," 1898), crossing the Kentucky River to select a site to build a fort and create a pioneer settlement that would become Madison County. His arrival opened the door for western expansion into an area that was still part of Virginia. (Kentucky became the fifteenth state in 1792.) William Chenault's article for *The Courier-Journal* (Louisville, Kentucky) on August 28, 1898, titled "Brave Defenders of Fort Boonesborough," gives a comprehensive account concerning the fort's history, named "Boonesborough" by Col. Richard Henderson to honor the legendary frontiersman. Chenault lists thirty-nine individuals who helped build *thirty cabins, including the block houses at each of its four corners.* The construction began in April 1775 and was completed in July 1776. Daniel Boone and his younger brother Squire Boone Jr. (1744–1815) are listed first, and ancestors Cuthbert (1745–1815) and "Enos" Combs (Ennis 1751–1828) are included. When their brother Captain Benjamin Combs (1749–1838) joined them, the Combs brothers became an integral part of the area's history, and mine.

My grandmother's parents, George Martin Webber (1832–1919) and Mariah Jane Combs (1848–1936) were both born in Clark County,

Kentucky. They were living in the Boonesborough area of Madison County when they married November 6, 1862. According to the County Marriage Record, Webber's "Occupation" was "Merchant" (eight months later, his Civil War record states he was a farmer), and this was his first marriage. There was a sixteen-year age difference between them; George was thirty years old, and Mariah Jane was only fourteen. A note is added to the marriage record about Edwin J. Combs (1818–1888). It states, "Edwin Combs father of bride gave his consent." The wedding took place at his home.

There are many fascinating records about the Webber and Combs lines, beginning with an article written by Emerson Miller for *The Courier-Journal*, Louisville, Kentucky, Dec. 7, 1959. The title "Mayflower Docked Later, Combs' Ancestors Pioneers" caught my attention. It provides a succinct look at a vast scope of American history and is shared for its descriptive account of our country's early years:

> The Combs family came to Kentucky when it was still "Indian country." It was among the first to blaze the trails, build rude log cabins, hew rough farms out of the wilderness, and hold back the Indians, depending primarily upon their long rifles and keen axes for food and shelter, and upon that most prized possession, the great family Bible, for spiritual nourishment.
>
> It is peculiarly fitting and appropriate, therefore, that when Governor-elect Bert T. Combs takes the oath of office Tuesday, it will be on his family's old Bible. And hovering in the background will be the ghosts of men in coonskin caps, others in kneebreeches and wearing periwigs, for the Combses were in America before the Mayflower dropped anchor off Plymouth Rock. They are the real "FFV's" (First Families of Virginia).
>
> John Combs came to Virginia on May 20, 1619, on the ship Marigold. Two of his grandsons, John and Joseph Combs, II, settled Stafford County, Virginia. John married Sythia "Seth" Bullitt, daughter of Capt. Benjamin Bullitt, and his wife Elizabeth Harrison, daughter of Thomas Harrison. They were the ancestors of the well-known Bullitt family of Louisville. Benjamin Combs, a son of John and Seth, settled in Clark County, Kentucky, in 1775.

John Combs Sr. (ca 1725–1786) and Seth Bullitt (ca 1731–1799) are my sixth Great-Grandparents, both born in Virginia. These families supported and served honorably in the Revolutionary War, but, as with George Washington (1732–1799) and Thomas Jefferson (1743–1826), slavery is also part of their history. Their story was uncovered while doing research for this chapter, with slavery a disappointing though not surprising discovery. I am a huge fan of the *PBS* television program *Finding Your Roots*, created and hosted by Dr. Henry Louis Gates Jr., Director of African American Studies and Research at Harvard, and I've often pondered my response to his follow-up question once guests learn their ancestors had slaves. How do they feel about this knowledge? Each person is disappointed and saddened, as I was, but the loathsome reality of slavery is understood to have existed in the heavily agrarian society of our ancestors. For the guests who descend from slaves, tears accompany profound pride in their family's resilience and strength to survive, even during the Jim Crow era from 1877 to the mid-1960s, when rights and freedoms were curtailed, suppressed, and denied. All guests and viewers of Dr. Gates's program share the deepest gratitude and respect for those who came before. We each marvel at our family's history, the comparative ease of our lives, and the blessing of our existence.

Since our country was established on religious and personal freedom, slavery was indeed a paradox. Thomas Jefferson (1743–July 4, 1826) was the author of America's founding document, the Declaration of Independence, adopted by the Continental Congress on July 4, 1776. He sought to address slavery's *deplorable entanglement* (Monticello), but passionate and conflicting viewpoints postponed a resolution. When the Declaration was written, Jefferson believed slavery would eventually impact our fledgling nation with *a civil war that would destroy the Union* (Monticello). Indeed, the Civil War (1861–1865) began eighty-five years later. Out of the tragedy of war, however, President Abraham Lincoln (1809–1865) signed the Emancipation Proclamation on January 1, 1863, giving freedom to the slaves, and America survived intact, though with keen losses on both the Union and Confederate sides. Today, America celebrates *Juneteenth* on June 19 to recognize the day in 1865 when the last slaves, who were living in Texas, received their freedom. In the Declaration of Independence, Jefferson had an encompassing vision for America when he penned one of the most profound statements ever written concerning human liberty:

> *We hold these truths to be self-evident, that all men are created equal, that they are endowed by their Creator with certain unalienable Rights, that among these are Life, Liberty and the pursuit of Happiness.*

The final sentence in the Declaration identifies the belief and spirit of the fifty-six men whose signatures acknowledged this truth in their establishment of a free and independent nation:

A SOUTHERN HERITAGE

And for the support of this Declaration, with a firm Reliance on the Protection of divine Providence, we mutually pledge to each other our Lives, our Fortunes, and our sacred Honor.

Massachusetts delegate John Hancock (1737–1793), who was the President of the Continental Congress during this momentous time, was the first to sign. His signature is bold and underlined with a flourish, a strong statement to Great Britain and the world, and an encouragement to the brave men who also signed their names:

> John Adams; Samuel Adams; Josiah Bartlett; Carter Braxton; Charles Carroll of Carrollton; Samuel Chase; Abraham Clark; George Clymer; William Ellery; William Floyd; Benjamin Franklin; Elbridge Gerry; Button Gwinnett; Lyman Hall; John Hancock; Benjamin Harrison; John Hart; Joseph Hewes; Thomas Heyward Jr.; William Hooper; Stephen Hopkins; Francis Hopkinson; Samuel Huntington; Thomas Jefferson; Francis Lightfoot Lee; Richard Henry Lee; Francis Lewis; Philip Livingston; Thomas Lynch Jr.; Thomas McKean; Arthur Middleton; Lewis Morris; Robert Morris; John Morton; Thomas Nelson Jr.; William Paca; Robert Treat Paine; John Penn; George Read; Caesar Rodney; George Ross; Dr. Benjamin Rush; Edward Rutledge; Roger Sherman; James Smith; Richard Stockton; Thomas Stone; George Taylor; Matthew Thornton; George Walton; William Whipple; William Williams; James Wilson; John Witherspoon; Oliver Wolcott; George Wythe

We are indebted to each signatory for committing his life to the cause of liberty, and to each soldier who fought in the Revolutionary War (April 19, 1775, to September 3, 1783). Our indebtedness extends as well to the wives and women who sacrificed for America's freedom. They provided aid to the soldiers through homemade provision and food and kept the home stable and functioning throughout the war and beyond, as women do.

There are many from both sides of my mother's family who fought in the Revolutionary War. Fourth Great-Grandfather Colonel Jonathan Evans (1730–1806) from Salisbury, Massachusetts, (the Remick line) was in the first encounter with the British. He was *Captain of a company of Minute Men, Col. James Frye's regt., which marched on the alarm of April 19, 1775* (*Massachusetts Soldiers and Sailors of The Revolutionary War*, 1891, 403). Known as "The Lexington Alarm," men responded to Paul Revere's urgent horseback ride the night before, made famous in the poem "Paul Revere's Ride" by Henry Wadsworth Longfellow (1807–1882), first published in 1861 in *The Atlantic Monthly*. Revere sounded the alarm so each village could prepare for the British, who were marching from Boston to Concord, Massachusetts, to seize military supplies and arrest opposing colonists. The British met resistance in Lexington, where 500 men in the colonial militia were waiting in a surprise encounter at dawn. The Revolutionary War began when a shot was fired from an unknown rifle, *the shot heard 'round the world*, as it was immortalized in a line from the Ralph Waldo Emerson (1803–1882) poem, "Concord Hymn" (1837). The minutemen fought valiantly but were outnumbered, with eight killed and ten wounded. The British were able to press forward, and when they arrived in Concord, no supplies were found. Reinforcements, however, had arrived and a battle took place. The British were forced back to South Boston, and the Siege of Boston began. There was no turning back for America. With profound gratitude, we celebrate their sacrifice and our country's 250th Anniversary, July 4, 2026.

Several interesting connections attach to this multi-layered history. Genealogical research always reveals surprising facts about our ancestry, and this happened when I learned about my relationship with Benjamin Franklin. His Grandparents Peter Folger and Mary Morrell had at least nine children (eight of them were born on Martha's Vineyard). As mentioned, I descend from their daughter Joanna (1645–1719), and Franklin descends from their daughter Abiah (1667–1752), who was born on Nantucket. With numerous children in the family, *many, many people today* are a first cousin to Benjamin Franklin, a humbling and thrilling connection waiting to be discovered.

A bit of research about Peter Folger uncovers his inspiring work with Rev. Thomas Mayhew Jr. (1620/21–1657), my ninth great-grandfather from Martha's Vineyard. They worked together as missionaries to the Wampanoag Indians who lived in southeastern Massachusetts and on Martha's Vineyard and Nantucket. These two men and Puritan missionary John Eliot (c.1604–1690) and others learned the oral Algonquian language, transcribed it into written form to establish literacy, and translated the Bible into the Algonquian language. Native bilinguals "James (the) Printer and Job Nesutan" (Fisher, *Peter Folger*, 2018) were invaluable in this endeavor. Coordinated and published by John Eliot in 1663, after Rev. Mayhew tragically died at sea on a voyage back to England, *The Bible, Up-Biblum* was the first Bible published in North America. Eliot's name is most associated with this work, also known as the *Eliot Indian Bible*. Together, these men and others who worked with them understood the truth of Romans 10:17 NKJV, *So then faith comes by hearing, and hearing by the word of God.*

Another connection involves my husband's family and the Civil War. His grandfather, Jasper Franklin Lee Patrick (1864-1930), was born during the Civil War in Wilkinsville, Union (now Cherokee) County, South Carolina. His father, John (1830-1865), was serving in the Confederacy and was tragically killed in the Battle of Petersburg, Virginia. Lee, as he was called, was raised by a single mother who never remarried, Mary Ann Peeler Patrick (1839-1904). When she died, Lee, at age forty-one, married twenty-two-year-old Minnie Blanton (1886-1957) a year later. They raised ten children, and their youngest child is my mother-in-law, Helen Patrick (1928-2015). Helen's father supported his large family as a rural mail carrier for the U.S. Postal Service, his transportation a horse and buggy. Helen married Jack Wirtz (1921-2016) in 1965. He was born in the Panama Canal Zone to William (1879-1943) and Elizabeth Theurer Wirtz (1882-1943), the tenth of eleven children. His father was an engineer in the construction of the Panama Canal, receiving the Roosevelt Medal #816 with three bars for his many years of service. The combination of a wide age span in grandparents, birth order, and a later marriage for his parents created a remarkable connection to American history for my husband William Patrick Wirtz. Born in 1967, he is only One Generation away from the Civil War.

The final connection also centers on the War Between the States and how divisions occurred within families over the issues of slavery and secession from the Union. Brothers fought on both sides of this conflict. This divide was especially true in the border state of Kentucky, which did not secede, although sixty-eight of 110 counties joined the Confederacy and set up their capital in the western city, Bowling Green. An example of familial division is revealed in the ancestral name "Benjamin Combs." Three men with this name, each from a different state, fought in the Civil War: one was in the Union Army, one served in the Confederate Army, and the third was a former slave named Benjamin Combs (his last name an indication of his previous owner) who belonged to the "U.S. Colored Troops, the 12th Regiment, U.S. Colored Heavy Artillery." This Benjamin Combs was held at the infamous Confederate prisoner-of-war camp, Andersonville Prison in Andersonville, Georgia, and died there on August 10, 1864.

Madison County, Kentucky, was pro-Union politically, and the men in that area were part of the 8th Kentucky Infantry Regiment. Great-Grandfather George Webber is listed in this regiment, 1863, and soon fought in various battles, including the Battle of Chickamauga and the Siege of Chattanooga. There were many encounters still to come over the next two years, but when Confederate General Robert E. Lee (1807–1870) surrendered to Union General Ulysses S. Grant (1822–1885) at Appomattox Court House, Virginia, on April 9, 1865, the war may have been officially over, but it took time for the news of Lee's surrender and the final cessation of fighting to occur. Five days after Appomattox, President Abraham Lincoln and his Kentucky-born wife, Mary Todd (1818–1882), attended Ford Theater in Washington, DC, to see the play *Our American Cousin*. As they sat in their theater box, John Wilkes Booth (1838–1865) shot Lincoln, who died the next day, April 15, 1865. His tragic death profoundly changed the course of history and made it more difficult to achieve the exhortation for compassion given in his brilliant and magnanimous second inaugural address on March 4, 1865:

> With malice toward none; and charity for all; with firmness in the right, as God gives us to see the right, let us strive on to finish the work we are in; to bind up the nation's wounds; to care for him who shall have borne the battle, and for his widow, and his orphan—to do all which may achieve and cherish a just and lasting peace among ourselves, and with all nations.

Once the Civil War was over, life began again for my Great-Grandparents George and Mariah Jane Combs Webber. For others, a happy reunion did not occur, which was sadly true for my husband's Great-Grandparents, John and Mary Ann Peeler Patrick. When the fighting stopped, most went home, but some never did, leaving us with the eternal question, "Why?"

> But as for me, I trust in You, O Lord;
> I say, "You are my God."
> My times are in Your hand.
> (Psalm 31:14–15 NKJV)

Chapter 19

Heading West

My Connection to Frances Webber Brubaker
This dear letter from my grandmother was a blessing that *God grant all the happiness* I was *looking forward to* in my marriage to
Arie E. Greenleaf.

My GRANDMOTHER FRANCES WEBBER Brubaker (1878–1975), affectionately called Fanny, recorded her life memories in February 1974 when she was ninety-six years old. Living in an assisted-living home in Phoenix, Arizona, her church friend, Bess Stenson, who visited regularly, made the delightful cassette tape recording one Sunday afternoon. Much history was shared, for much had been lived.

President Thomas Jefferson doubled the size of the United States in 1803 when he paid France $15 million (close to $28 million with interest) for the territory stretching west from the Mississippi River to the Rocky Mountains, and south from Canada to New Orleans. This transaction was known as the Louisiana Purchase. It was a fulfillment of Jefferson's vision to expand the country westward through landownership, accomplished through the perseverance and hard work of farm families, about whom he wrote, *Those who labor in the earth are the chosen people of God* (History.com). He commissioned Captain Meriwether Lewis (1774–1809) and Lieutenant William Clark (1770–1838) to explore this purchased land through an expedition called the Corps of Discovery. Leaving St. Louis in May 1804, Lewis and Clark traversed land and river in a tremendous quest to reach the Pacific Ocean, which they did via the Columbia River one and a half years later, arriving back in St. Louis in September 1806. They recorded every astonishing thing they saw and experienced, their monumental adventure setting the stage for fulfilling the "Manifest Destiny" (journalist John O'Sullivan, 1845) that would inspire America to populate the vast land of the Louisiana Purchase and beyond. This Westward Expansion was accelerated through the building of railroads across the Continent, and through a government program designed to help individuals acquire their own property.

The U.S. Congress passed the Homestead Act and President Abraham Lincoln signed it into law in May 1862. One hundred-sixty acres of public land could be claimed by pioneer settlers seeking a new place to live and raise a family. After paying the filing fee, a five-year commitment to living on the land, constructing a dwelling, and raising crops was required to receive the deed. This was an enticing opportunity for farm families, but, sadly, losses from drought and crop failure tragically ended some dreams. The second option was to live on the land and farm it for six months, then pay the government $1.25 per acre. According to the Kansas Historical Society, the state experienced its greatest population increase in the twenty-five years following the Civil War through this opportunity

While the lure of free or (relatively) inexpensive land available through the Homestead Act brought numerous settlers into the wide-open plains of the Midwest, some just came. Among those pioneers were the Webber, Combs, and Brubaker families. They made their way westward through Ohio, Indiana, Illinois, Missouri, and into the Great Plains of Kansas and on into Nebraska for Noah and Elizabeth. Their son, my Grandfather Richard Brubaker (1879–1964), is Fanny's husband, and he was born in Beatrice, Gage County, Nebraska, where they farmed for over twenty years before moving and ultimately settling in Sawyer, Kansas, in 1902. The western trek for all these families included farming along the way, sometimes for a year or two in one place. Children were born in each of these six Heartland states, and sometimes parents faced the death and parting of a beloved child (the Brubaker's first daughter, Mary Ann, was about ten months old when she died in Illinois). The ability for each family to face difficult and exhausting challenges and keep moving forward in faith and trust is their testimony, one that speaks to the resilient strength of the American spirit.

Our ancestors are nothing short of awe-inspiring, for they are models of determined endurance and acceptance in the hard, while demonstrating grace and gratitude in the joy.

Several years after the Civil War, George and Mariah Jane Combs Webber set out for Burlington, Coffey County, Kansas, arriving in 1873 and settling near her father, Edwin Combs, who had arrived a year earlier. Edwin lived there seventeen years when he tragically died from *blood poisoning* from *a locust thorn* which *accidentally pierced his thigh*, as stated in his obituary in *The Burlington Republican* (Burlington, Kansas) on Friday, January 25, 1889. *He bore his suffering with the fortitude of a hero,* it added, while also defining Edwin as a *kind husband, loving father and honored friend.* His obituary confirms America's movement and character:

> [Edwin Combs] was born in Kentucky, where his early life was spent in hard labor. There he learned the lessons of early rising, honesty and integrity that surrounded him in old age . . . He moved to Missouri in 1870, where he remained for two years, and then came to Coffey County, where he has since lived, an honored and respected citizen. A man who was never idle, he never forgot the neighbor who was in need. Truly believing that charity is the noblest of Christian graces, no one, whether known or stranger, friend or foe, was permitted to go hungry or empty-handed from his door.

Like her father, Mariah Jane and George had a married life that mirrors the story of America's movement and experience in the last half of the nineteenth century. Their first three children were born in Kentucky, 1866 to 1870. A daughter was born in Missouri in 1872. Then six were born in Kansas, including my Grandmother Frances in 1878, who states in her cassette recording, "I was born on the farm, seven miles from Burlington, Coffey County, Kansas . . . the sixth child of ten children, six boys and four girls." When Fanny was eight years old, the Webber family moved to Sawyer, where two more children were born, completing this family of twelve.

A fascinating note about pioneering life and community growth is expressed in the obituary for my Great-Grandfather George Martin Webber, found in the *Sawyer News* (Sawyer, Kansas) on Friday, Aug. 1, 1919:

> When he came here he moved into a dug-out, that being about the only sort of homes here then. He immediately built what was then regarded as a commodious farm home. While most of his years were devoted to farming, he at times engaged in the mercantile

business. He built the first business building and put in the first stock of goods at Sawyer and was Sawyer's first postmaster.

With both sets of great-grandparents and their children moving to Sawyer, the stage was set for an addition to the family tapestry. These inspired decisions brought Richard and Frances together, and they were married in 1904, two years after the Brubaker family arrived. On the cassette recording, my grandmother explains that prior to her marriage, she "attended the [Sawyer] village school through eighth grade," and then took classes at Nickerson College for three terms. She proudly added that at age seventeen she "passed the teacher's exam with a high score . . . in the nineties." Fanny's graduation picture shows her seated and a friend standing, both wearing long, stylish white dresses with leg o'mutton sleeves, each holding a rosette ribbon with the year 95 boldly printed on the single streamer. [Since we share a cherished physical resemblance, this picture is framed and on my antique dresser to enjoy every day.] When Grandma began teaching the primary grades, she was "seven miles from home and boarded with a family." She taught at several different schools for a total of nine terms before she and Richard were married.

My grandparents had two sons, Bernard and my father Kenneth. They lived thirty years on the farm in Hugoton, in southwestern Kansas, less than fifty miles from the Oklahoma Panhandle border. They survived the drought-stricken, Dust Bowl years of the "Dirty Thirties," when the fertile, Midwestern farmland dried up and blew away in towering black dust clouds which blocked the sun and choked and buried everything in their path. Nothing was safe, including one's health, for dust particles caused Dust Pneumonia, resulting in death and permanent lung damage. No barrier could keep all the dust out. A multi-year lack of rain combined with uninformed farming practices that depleted and destroyed the topsoil, resulting in a devastated farm economy. Families walked away from their farms and the land they loved, for nothing was left. Many of the migrants who went to California were from Oklahoma, and the influx prompted the derogatory name "Okies." All were considered "Dust Bowl Refugees" (Smithsonian American Art Museum.com). In 1936, journalist Ernie Pyle (1900–1945), who became a Pulitzer Prize winner for his World War II reporting, visited an area in southwestern Kansas just over the Oklahoma border, where my grandparents were, and wrote in June 1936, *If you would like to have your heart broken, just come out here. This is the dust-storm country. It is the saddest land I have ever seen* (Legends of America.com).

The drought finally lifted toward the end of the decade, and the food and manufacturing needed to win World War II brought a turnaround for farmers and the country. My grandparents had earned a well-deserved break, and in 1945 planned a month-long trip to Phoenix, Arizona, a visit that forever changed their lives. When my grandmother's severely arthritic hands improved in the warm, dry climate, and once again she was able to do everyday chores and "take care of my husband," they turned the farm over to son Bernard and bought a home in Phoenix. They rarely traveled to St. Louis to see us, but when we drove across the country on Route 66 to California to see Aunt Agnes and Uncle Jim, we always stopped to see them. Memories of our times together are distinct and precious, as memories with grandparents usually are. After Grandpa died in 1964 from Parkinson Disease, Grandma moved to an assisted living home and died eleven years later. Fortunately, the cassette recording was completed a year and a half before she died. The tape made its way to Hugoton, and when my mother visited the farm in 1976, she was asked to add a few words at the end. She states the reason for the recording, "So all can have this tape of their grandmother's voice," but hearing my mother's lovely voice is an added blessing.

Modern technological advancement made the cassette tape recorder obsolete, but in its day, it was used to easily record and preserve family history for later generations. Listening to my grandmother's voice as she recounts her teaching and farming days is a priceless experience. When she joins visitors in singing "The Old Rugged Cross," as I did, tears are unavoidable. When she ends the tape recording with her signature blessing, "Good-bye, Honeys, God bless you," the power of the listening moment overwhelms with a gratitude and love that is inexpressible. The essence of my Dear Grandmother's faith and personality is clear in her life and in the prayers and good wishes in the letter I received a month before my marriage to Arie E. Greenleaf.

Letter ~ Frances Webber Brubaker, 1967

Monday, July 10 / 1967

Good morning, My Darling Ann:

A <u>warm</u> summer day here, but I suspect it is there, too. One disagreeable factor you have that we don't, is the high humidity. Our humidity here is <u>usually</u> very low.

Honey, I just know how happy you are, anticipating your marriage. God grant <u>all</u> the happiness you are looking forward to.

I am feeling fine this morning. Still in #10, but guess they will move me to #1, at their convenience. <u>Whatever</u> deal is made, will be O.K. by me.

The verses on the card, I thought, would be good logic for you and Arie to read together. They sounded <u>so</u> <u>true</u>.

I do hope your plans will all be fulfilled. I am sure your dad will be a proud father, escorting his daughter to her bridegroom,* but he will miss you, honey, and so will mom.

Here is love, a kiss, a prayer from,
A Doting Grandma

*One of the pictures in my wedding album is my dear dad escorting me down the aisle. I'm smiling and completely oblivious to what he was feeling. My father was struggling to maintain his composure, the tears in his eyes evoking my own.

AUGUST

CHAPTER 20 . . . A NEW ENGLAND HERITAGE

My Connection to Charlotte Remick Brubaker
Letter: Charlotte Remick Brubaker, 1972

Chapter 20

A New England Heritage

My Connection to Charlotte Remick Brubaker
This letter reflects a mother's cherished love and prayer for her daughter
who has just given birth to a grandson, *I know he is a darling*,
a continuation of a grateful heritage.

MOST OF US HAVE some understanding of our immediate heritage, with perhaps some knowledge about the Great-Grands of our ancestry, but beyond that, little is known. As mentioned, taking a genealogy class at Nicolet College in Rhinelander, Wisconsin, in 2001 forever changed and broadened my life. Twenty-five years later, this off and on journey has uncovered a vast knowledge of profoundly astonishing, humbling, and thrilling family history. Also, abundantly clear in this journey of discovery is how *our family's story is simply a reflection of everyone else's astonishing American story and the depth of our connection to each other.*

My initial visit to the Wisconsin State Historical Society building on the UW campus was simply the beginning of an unfolding adventure that still astounds. Subsequent visits uncovered information about my mother's ancestry, which quickly revealed a deep tie to New England, especially to Massachusetts, Maine, and New Hampshire. As every genealogist knows, and I soon discovered, each family surname leads to another line and another, and on it goes, making research about one's ancestry truly unending. Every trip to Madison made that clear.

One trip uncovered a connection to the local historian, genealogist, and author John Brooks Threlfall (1920-2017) who wrote *The Ancestry of Thomas Bradbury (1611-1695) and His Wife Mary (Perkins) Bradbury (1615-1700) of Salisbury, Massachusetts* (Second Edition-1995). Thomas and Mary Bradbury are my eighth Great-Grandparents, and Mr. Threlfall and I descend from two of their daughters. In February 2002, a fascinating afternoon was spent at John's home, where I purchased his masterful, six-hundred-page tome of dedicated research and study and took a picture of him autographing his remarkable work. Much was discussed that day about the Bradbury/Pekins families, including their European roots, thoroughly detailed in his book. Their lines trace back to Charlemagne (ca 742/748–814), the "Father of Europe" who was crowned the Holy Roman Emperor by Pope Leo III on December 25, 800. John created a large chart of this ancestry and kindly gave me a copy, which I framed. He also emphatically stated, "Anyone with Western European ancestry probably has Charlemagne in their family tree, for he had many wives, concubines, and children."

The other astonishing piece of information about the Bradbury family concerns Mary and the infamous Salem Witch Trials (January 1692–1693). Mary was age seventy-seven in July 1692 when she was accused of being a witch. According to William Carr's testimony (Threlfall, *Bradbury*, 3), about thirteen years prior, he and his brother and their "honored father" (George) were riding by the Bradbury home and saw Mary enter a gate and go around a corner, when "a blue boar ... darted out of [the] gate." William explained that his father's horse "stumbled," and the father asked, "Boys, what did you see?" They both answered, "A blue boar." Apparently, the boar disappeared, for William stated he, "saw it no more," implying the boar had either been conjured or had been Mary herself.

This dear woman was also accused and found guilty of bewitching William's brother, John, who "became melancholy and at times insane." The trial revealed the father had forbidden him to marry because of "his youth," an indication the son's illness and death were not from a spell cast by Mary. The son's object of affection was Mary's daughter, Jane Bradbury (1645-1729/30), who had rejected him and married Henry True (1644/5-1735). Jane and Henry True are my seventh great-grandparents. The intriguing reality about genealogy is that if one person is missing in our family tree, we're not here. If Jane had married John Carr . . . or if Mary had accepted George Carr's marriage proposal before she married Thomas Bradbury . . . (Berry, "The Witchcraft Trial," 2015, *Genealogy Magazine*.com).

According to William's testimony, there had been "some differences" between the families before the witch trials started, which shows how any tragedy, dispute, rejection, or imagined incident fed into the witchcraft hysteria consuming the Massachusetts Colony. Defended by her daughter-in-law's father, Major Robert Pike, Mary received numerous *testimonies to her excellent character* from her husband and family, and from *one hundred and eighteen of [her] neighbors*, who signed a statement of support that begins with, *[her life] was such as becomes the gospel*. Despite their best efforts, Mary *was convicted with four others who were executed but somehow she escaped execution* (Threlfall, *Bradbury*, 3). After learning this story, I determined I would never share Great-Grandmother Mary's terrible ordeal without including her personal declaration of faith and innocence (Threlfall, *Bradbury*, 2):

> I am wholly innocent of any such wickedness through the goodness of God who has kept me hitherto. I am the servant of Jesus Christ and have given myself up to him as my only Lord and Savior, and to the contempt and defiance of the devil and all his works as horrid and detestable and have accordingly endeavored to frame my life and conversations according to the rules of his holy word, and in that faith and practice, resolve by the help and assistance of God to continue to my life's end. For the truth of what I say, I humbly refer myself to my brethren and neighbors that know me, and unto the searcher of all hearts for the truth and uprightness of my heart therein (human frailties and Unavoidable excepted) of which I bitterly complain every day.

In the end, more than two hundred people were accused of witchcraft. Twenty were executed, all but one by hanging. Mary lived another eight years, long enough to experience the state's remorse about the trials when, three years before she died, the General Court ordered a day for soul-searching and fasting. The trials were declared unlawful in 1702, and nine years later the heirs received financial restitution along with the restoration of their loved one's reputation. In 1957, a formal apology for the witchcraft trials was issued by the Massachusetts legislature, with the lone person left to be exonerated receiving her pardon in 2022 (Blumberg, "A Brief History," 2022, *Smithsonian Magazine*.com).

Continuous genealogical investigation is usually difficult to maintain, but *Ancestry* has proved the most invaluable for easy, comprehensive research and is my main source. Other genealogical websites, like *MyHeritage* or *FamilySearch*, provide additional insight and confirmation, and searches on the internet and *WikiTree* are helpful. There will often be discrepancies and conflicts that require additional study. Still, wonders are ever waiting to be discovered, and an in-depth pursuit can reveal gratifying information. This occurred when studying my Scottish ancestry in 2022, and I learned Daniel Stewart from Martha's Vineyard was my seventh great-grandfather. A deeper study led to the astonishing fact that *fifty-five of my maternal, multi-great-grandparents were born on Martha's Vineyard*. Naming the many family lines demonstrates the vast interconnectedness of our nation and is an encouragement for others to pursue their ancestral roots. They include Allen, Athearn, Butler, Cathcart, Chase, Cottle, Luce, Manter, Mayhew, Merry, Norton, Pease, Presbury, Skiffe, Stewart, Tilton, West, Whitten, and Wollen.

Descendants of many of these families still live on Martha's Vineyard.* My Great-Great-Grandmother Catherine Luce (1790–1867) was the last of my direct family line to be born there. Her parents, along with some in the Manter family, and others moved to Maine, where Catherine met and married True Remick (1789–1863) from Tamworth, New Hampshire. Their son John (1833–1893) married Malvina Patterson (1838–1918), daughter of Caleb (1806–1883) and Caroline Manter Patterson (1814–1889). John and Malvina are the parents of Grandfather Benjamin Luce Remick and his brother John True Remick (1869–1910).

The connection to Tamworth, New Hampshire, continues today through my fourth Great-Grandfather Captain Enoch Remick (1730–1800), who came from Kittery, Maine, and established a farm that is still operational. His descendant, Dr. Edwin Remick (1866–1900), who is my first cousin three times removed, was the local doctor who ran his practice on the first floor of their residence. His son Dr. Edwin Crafts Remick (1903–1993) maintained the practice and established a foundation to *preserve the agricultural way of life in New Hampshire*, known today as the Remick Country Doctor Museum & Farm. Open to the public, its website www.newsite.remickmuseum.org explains their mission:

> Welcome to Remick . . . a historic site and working farm, featuring exhibits, gardens, walking trails and more. Visit to explore 200+

years of NH's agricultural traditions combined with the unique story of two country doctors.

Another revelation occurred through my Martha's Vineyard study, an unearthing of that most curious of genealogical questions: Does my ancestry connect to the Mayflower? It was thrilling to discover my ninth Great-Grandfather is Richard Warren (abt. 1578–1628), Mayflower Passenger and Signer of the Mayflower Compact. His story includes his participation in The First Encounter, a surprise skirmish with Native Americans in December 1620, where thankfully no one was hurt. He survived the first brutal winter into spring (1620–21) when nearly half of the 104 Mayflower passengers and crew died. Richard was a Pilgrim at the First Thanksgiving, where only fifty-three were alive to celebrate including, shockingly, only four of the original eighteen adult women. He welcomed his wife Elizabeth Walker (1583–1673) and their five daughters to Plymouth Colony in 1623. Two sons were born, but, sadly, Richard died within a year of the birth of his last child. His death is recorded in *New England's Memorial* written by Nathaniel Morton, 1669, who states, *This year [1628] died Mr. Richard Warren, who was an useful instrument and during his life bare a deep share in the difficulties and troubles of the first settlement of the Plantation of New Plymouth* (Caleb Johnson's mayflowerhistory.com). Warren's seven children all grew into adulthood, married, and had large families. *His Mayflower descendants are in the millions*, some of the most numerous of all the original passengers, and they include President Ulysses S. Grant (thehistoryjunkie.com), making Grant my sixth cousin three times removed. When you consider the *immense number of people* who connect to Richard Warren alone, the scope of our connectedness is astounding.

One final note demonstrates the mystery of inherited traits and practices. John and Malvina Patterson Remick and their two-year old son Benjamin moved to Waverly, Iowa, making way for the family tapestry to begin its Midwestern story. Great-Grandmother Malvina had interests and routines that mirror mine, as discovered through a scrapbook she created with newspaper clippings spanning the early 1900s until her death in 1918. It's an amazing compilation of stories; history; family weddings; and of articles written by her son, John. He was born in Waverly and became a successful teacher and Superintendent of Schools, dying young at age forty-one from tuberculosis. All these notices have been carefully clipped and glued into the scrapbook, where I'm sure tears fell as she added the obituaries for her husband and son. How did those years pass so quickly?

Malvina herself died tragically, her obituary and other articles revealing her daily routine at the time of her death, a routine that is my own. Posted on the *Find a Grave* website, two newspaper clippings from January 1918 tell the story of a woman of deep faith who loved and cared for her home. She swept her porch every day, even when it snowed, as I do. Malvina was sweeping and was overcome with a dizzy spell, fell off the porch, and died from exposure. Her neighbor found her *lying upon the broom*, covered with snow. While this was upsetting to learn, it was also astonishing to discover through an obituary that I had inherited a daily habit from my great-grandmother. Now, when I commence my morning sweeping, regardless of the weather, I think of dear Malvina, grateful for her inherited ways, yet sad for the way she died.

*[For a unique and engaging presentation of Martha's Vineyard, Susan Branch's inspiring autobiography, *Martha's Vineyard, Isle of Dreams*, Spring Street Publishing, 2016, is highly recommended. www.susanbranch.com]

Letter ~ Charlotte Remick Brubaker, 1972

August 1972

Dearest Ann, Arie & <u>Todd</u>—

I'm so happy Todd arrived early and that everything went so well. You sounded just wonderful on the phone, Ann—a little tired naturally—but mighty happy, and I know Arie is thrilled too. 8 lbs.—that's a good size—I know he is a darling. Take some pictures, Arie. You'll probably hear that often from me!

As I mentioned—I wrote a note last nite, saying not to be surprised if the baby was late in arriving—as is often the case with the first baby! Tore that note up in a hurry this a.m.

Have called a few people. Laverne was going to call Gina [my friend, Ginny Burch]. Will try to call Jan [Schnieders]. Don't know if she's here yet or not.

I'll write more later. Rest, Ann—you'll be busy when you get home. Give little Todd a big hug for Grandma —I'm surely looking forward to seeing him—and Mom & Dad too.

May the good Lord be kind to young Todd and allow him to grow up to be a blessing to you both.

Love always,
Grandma, Grandpa,
& Uncle Pete

SEPTEMBER

CHAPTER 21 ... MARRIAGE, BIRTH, AND FRIENDSHIPS

My Connection to Family and Friends: Jane Romack, Karin Wooten, and Leanna Sain
Letter: Jane Romack, 2014

Chapter 21

Marriage, Birth, and Friendships

My Connection to Family and
Friends: Jane Romack, Karin Wooten, and Leanna Sain
These letters and messages beautifully convey the *blessings* received
from family and friends, and the hope we receive in our *struggles*.

SEPTEMBER HAS ALWAYS BEEN a month for meaningful correspondence. It follows a busy August when weddings and births have taken place, and an overflow of good wishes have been received. Plus, it's my birthday month. Over the years, many delightful cards and letters from both months have been tucked away for their visual and inspirational appeal. This chapter shares some of the universal good wishes and blessings that uplift in the eloquence of deeply felt language.

One carry-over from August connects to the birth of our son, Arie Todd, and is a grandfather's deep expression of love and faith:

> August 1972
> 7:20 a.m.
> Dear Ann & Arie:
>   Congratulations!!! Think you're happy and proud. You should see Todd's grandpa.

I'll say this for the first time to you. I can't explain to you my feeling exactly. So you will have to wait a few years until you are Grandparents.

I'll have to admit this. When I heard the good news last night, I went immediately to the workshop to finish the cradle. It had been completed except for rubbing and setting the color tone. Can't you just imagine the special feeling that has been rubbed into each stroke.

And the great thing about it is that the love, good wishes, concern, hopes for Todd's future, and all the worthwhile things that go into prayers & meditation.

And the final close of these thoughts when the last touch is made to the cradle, "Thanks be to our God" for all of His goodness, mercy, and love. Great and mighty is His power and love.

And we pray His special blessing on this gift from Heaven.

Your Father

Could a grandfather's loving heart be any clearer? This grandson belonged to Arie, his eldest and firstborn son, who had experienced deep sadness when his first wife died. Usually, weddings and births unite us with joy, although sometimes there are shadows. Sandra would not survive her cancer, and there would be no grandchildren from their union. After Arie and I were wed in August 1967, the hopes for a long and happy marriage, and perhaps a grandchild, were felt once again (although it was five years before our son was born). A month after our wedding, I received a very special note from Arie's mother, who was thankful her son had found love again. The beautiful flower painting on the front of the card is identified on the back: *"Zinnias" by the celebrated artist Lillian Grow*. Mother's dear message still brings a smile:

N. Indiana Ave.
Peoria, Illinois
September 12, 1967
Dear Mrs. Greenleaf,

I just wanted you to know how happy I am that you are a member of our family. There is so much pleasure to look forward to. Won't it be fun?

I've grown to be quite fond of your husband. It is pure pleasure to see you together.

Lovely wishes,
Mrs. Greenleaf

Mother and I certainly did have fun throughout the thirty-seven years we were together before she died, eight months after Arie's death. Mary was widowed twice during those years, but her determination to continue embracing the joy of living made an impact and helped me through my own loss. We learn from each other how to live life, especially how to have courage when we feel broken. The Scottish expression, "Some things are better felt than telt" is also stated, "Lessons are caught not taught." Our observant nature makes us ever aware and ever learning. My wonderful mother and my two dear mothers-in-law modeled how to be loving, committed, attentive, sacrificial, faithful, and true to the Lord. They were kind and generous, and they expressed their love in articulate, meaningful ways. Mary and her second husband, Bob Campen, sent a *Leanin' Tree* birthday card to Arie for his 50th birthday in 1989, a lifelike painting of Mallard ducks landing in a marshy pond, identified "Southern Tradition" by Harry Curieux Adamson. She tenderly wrote:

> I can remember your father's 50th birthday. We had a fine family celebration.
>
> But what I remember most was his saying that his 50th birthday marked a re-newing of life.
>
> How sweet the birds sang. How beautiful the sky, a deeper appreciation of life. I wish you these gifts.
>
> Love,
> Mother & Bob

The last birthday card I ever received from my faithful mom, who never forgot to extend her loving wishes, was received two months before she died at age ninety-two. After taking a week to drive from Northern Wisconsin to our new home on Davis Mountain in Hendersonville, North Carolina, Arie and I moved in on Friday, November 2002, and my mother died on Monday. These were pre-cellphone days, so we were out of touch during the trip, and then I couldn't reach her. My cousin Charlotte Ann explained Mom was in the hospital. Thankfully, we were able to talk and pray one last time. In September, she had sent a *Gibson* greeting card with an adorable "Mother" bunny in her white apron standing by a wheelbarrow filled with flowers, a bouquet in her hand. The card states, *Daughter, on your Birthday and always . . . Happiness grows wherever you are*:

> 9–14–02
> Dear Ann—

SEPTEMBER

> After lunch today, Charlotte Ann & I looked for cards. The supply where we went was not very attractive—sorry to say [except this one].
>
> Just want you to know Ann how much I appreciate all the wonderful things you have done for me over the years.
>
> Have a great Birthday—you are a dear person whom I love very much.
>
> Mom

Treasured words, but in my heart, I know I could have done more! Can we ever receive expressions of love from our parents and not wish we had been more attentive . . . more loving . . . more caring . . . more grateful . . . more involved . . . more aware of time passing . . . less consumed by our own lives? Is it ever any other way? Probably not. Words and actions left unsaid and undone may be regretful, but time moves forward anyway. This is simply part of living because few of us will ever think we "did enough." This holds true in reverse, for as parents, we will always have our regrets. In the end, regardless of how inadequate we feel we've been, sincere love remains the difference-maker, and our sorrowful hearts are soothed by compassion and understanding toward ourselves and others. The wisdom of the Word conveys this truth, *Most important of all, continue to show deep love for each other, for love covers a multitude of sins* (1 Peter 4:8 NLT).

A very special writers' group was formed on September 7, 2010, Weavers of Words (WOW). Carol Guthrie Heilman, author of numerous books, including *Becoming Hattie Mae* (2025), had approached several of us at church to see if we'd be interested, and we were. We met at my home every month for the first year, branching out as we went along. Our friendships grew as we shared our lives and needs, which became as important as the encouragement we gave each other. Carol, Judy Dearing (*Chrissy's Moments*, 2013), Leanna Sain (Southern suspense), Karin Wooten (inspirational short stories), and I made up the initial group, with poet Betsy Thorne (*Measured Words*, 2019) a long-distance member. People moved away, and there have been additions: Kathy Pierson (freelance writer) and Sunny Lockwood (*Cruising Panama's Canal*, 2013, and other *Cruising* adventures, who is also the author Merikay McLeod, *The Day After His Crucifixion*, 2025). Time passed and change occurred, so we no longer meet regularly, but some of us gather occasionally to encourage and rekindle the joy of our fellowship. In a keepsake note from 2019, Karin describes the essence of our friendship, the essence of all deep friendships:

Don't we always say the same thing to each other? How is it that it's always exciting and a thrill to see you [and WOW]? The love is always there, the joy, the respect, the friendship, the awe of talents & gifts, and the tender hearts woven together by the same Spirit. What a treasure to be a friend of yours!

Love you so, so much!

Karin

From this dear group of friends, Leanna Sain and I have developed an extraordinary friendship. We have become sisters, and more. Every Friday morning (or another day, if busy), we meet at my house. Wedding silver paired with Depression Glass or fine china, along with seasonal mugs, napkins, and décor, make our time together festive. We settle back, put our feet up, and over coffee and treats, we share life and prayer. While it's our "therapy" time, and tears are sometimes shed, it's also our writers' time, for we discuss our books and writing endeavors, a sounding board and advisor to each other. Leanna has been the most prolific writer in our group. Her award-winning Amelia Island and G.R.I.T.S. series (Girls Raised in the South), now eleven books and counting, are a great read with their mysterious and intriguing plots, some with a time travel theme. With covers that identify the main characters, the guy adorable and the woman enchanting, her books captivate with their eye-catching appeal. Many heartfelt thank-you notes have been written between us over the years, the same message back and forth—how blessed we are:

> My sweet, sweet friend, what would I do w/o you? I'm so thankful and I thank God. He brought you into my life because He knew I'd need you. I consider you my best girlfriend & I've never really had that kind of friendship before . . . never realized I *needed* that until you.
>
> I love you like a big sister . . . better than a sister! [I am twelve years older than Leanna.]
>
> Thank you for our "coffee dates" every Friday morning. They're what get me through to the next one!

Jane Romack and I have been friends since 1978. Arie and I moved back to Bloomington, Illinois, and bought a house on Taylors Avenue, and she lived down the street. Our sons were taking swimming lessons at a nearby park, and we met as mothers sitting poolside. We quickly discovered we had similar interests (reading, walking, sewing) and immediately became friends. Learning her September birthday was exactly one week before mine [she is seven years older] united our hearts forever. While gifts are sometimes sent, we always send a card, usually two girls enjoying life together, like the one designed by *Leanin' Tree*, identified: *Yankee Gallery, "Autumn Ride" by Robert Sarsony*. Two friends are riding bicycles in an autumn wood, and beneath the painting Jane wrote, *"Us" in September.* The card's message is true, *Friendships born of the heart last through the years and across the miles.* Jane still eloquently expresses the joy we discovered in each other, all those many, many years ago:

> I always think <u>multiple</u> thoughts of you when September comes.
> How wonderful that we share our birthday month!
> Celebrating our years of friendship.
> Love every day . . .
> Thank you for another beautiful birthday card.
> You have always made my life more fabulous, through many years!
> Heart to heart forever . . .

Our hearts have, indeed, shared many life moments, including the same sorrow, and the same joy. Jane's husband, Terry, fought a valiant battle against cancer and died in 2013, and Arie, after his year-long cancer battle, died in 2004. Jane and I were each given the wonderful gift of a second happy marriage, her Rick McGraw and my Patrick Wirtz. The following is an insightful excerpt from Jane's 2014 letter, written a year after Terry's death. The choices she made in handling her grief encourage us to choose a positive path forward. Her words demonstrate that life does go on, though at times hard and overwhelming; that other people's grief can give us perspective on our own struggles; and that expressing our compassion never goes unnoticed.

Letter – Jane Romack, 2014

September 14, 2014

Dear Ann,

Thank you very much for sending your thoughtful birthday towel [an autumn kitchen hand-towel I made with a crocheted top], card, and affectionate note. I was so happy to hear from you, as I think of you often. When I read your letter today, I immediately wanted to call you.

I have not kept up with correspondence and cards; as you know, there are so many business details to manage—and that's about all I get done. I've been working on Vanguard papers for 7 months. Some days I despair of being finished—but I'm almost done. I have a wonderful second cousin, accountant and investment friend to help me, but still . . .

As you noted, we are approaching the date of Terry's death last year—September 19, and my heart has been heavy. I know the day will come and the day will go, and I'll be OK because God is with me every day. Thank you for acknowledging that his death date is near.

I experience abundant blessings every day, and I'm grateful every day. *Sometimes when I struggle, I thank God for all that was, all that is, and all that will be.* [my italics] A few Sundays ago, I felt the abundance of blessings and I began a Word document for blessings of the day. I enjoy adding to that every day or so . . .

Since Terry's death, I am immediately an "older woman," and that's where I fit socially. Several widows at Calvary have begun a "widow's group," but I can't even think about being part of such a group, even though it might be fun and helpful. I know you understand this difficulty.

I have begun going to the OSF (Order of St. Francis) bereavement group, and eventually I have come to like it. The value is not "instant healing" for myself, but listening to the other grieving stories helps me have perspective on my own . . .

I have the blessing of many friends—and a grateful heart. You, Ann, continue to be one of my greatest blessings.

Love and friendship,
JaneR

OCTOBER

CHAPTER 22 . . . BETWEEN THE LINES

My Connection to William Eugene Greenleaf
Letter: William Eugene Greenleaf, 1972

Chapter 22

Between the Lines

My Connection to William Eugene Greenleaf
This letter is a profound statement of life and the recognition that in hard times, *love for each other* will be our *sunshine in the dark*.

THE THOUGHTFUL LETTER RECEIVED from Arie's father in October 1972 defines the character of this loving man. His response to our letter to him, and to other letters he had received, demonstrates his contemplative, positive nature. *I like to read between the lines*, he wrote, and his perceptions are a literary treasure of choice in the face of change. And we were facing a major change.

As I've shared, Arie was unemployed the day our son was born in August 1972. His counseling position had been terminated, and he had been desperately trying to find employment, but nothing had come through. His upcoming job interview with the counseling center in Trempealeau County in southwestern Wisconsin, provided some hope. Thankfully, he was offered the job and began work several weeks later. The next two months, Arie came home on weekends and was helpful, but I was mostly alone to pack our house and take care of our newborn son. He took a room at a boarding house and looked for a place for us to rent, but nothing was available. Finally, we bought a house in Whitehall, sold our Rhinelander home, and moved in at the end of October. These are simple statements. The reality was hard.

Nobody's American story goes smoothly. At some point along the way, our youthful idealism, regardless of our age, faces disappointment and challenge. We experience loss, heartache, war, and now, in the twenty-first century, devastatingly severe weather. It seems that storms are occurring with an increasing intensity across our nation and world, leaving unfathomable destruction and despair. Hurricane Helene roared into Western North Carolina on September 27, 2024, a cataclysmic event that devoured life, property, and communities. I posted my thoughts on Facebook:

> The destruction that occurred still overwhelms with a sorrow that is inexpressible. I have used the word "heartbreaking" to describe what has happened but have decided that word is too tame. This Once in 1000 Year event is simply Soul Shattering. The lives carried away in the extreme flooding or caught in the horrific mudslides throughout WNC is a tragedy both overwhelming and incomprehensible. Businesses, homes, and communities have lost everything. Everything.
>
> Despite the horror and losses that have occurred, however, faith will forever bring hope, our Lord will forever bring peace, and His love will forever be demonstrated through the tremendous outpouring of prayer, help, support, and love that is given. For every hurricane, tornado, flood, mudslide, wind-damage, or any other natural event that occurs anywhere, I pray with a depth of compassion for those impacted, hurting for their losses in a way I never have before.
>
> For every kindness given to those in need, God bless you, for you are loved and appreciated beyond your understanding. Thank you.

Nine months and one week later, July 4, 2025, a similar heart-wrenching and horrific disaster occurred in the Hill Country of Central and South Texas. Torrential rainfall caused the Guadalupe River to rise a reported twenty-six feet in forty-five minutes, and perhaps even more. The overpowering flood waters wiped away homes, campsites, businesses, and most tragically of all, at least 135 people, including thirty-seven children. A month later, two were still missing, including one child. Camp Mystic (1926), an all-girls, Christian summer camp in Kerr County, located near the Guadalupe River, received the brunt of the disaster fatalities, with the loss of twenty-seven mostly eight- and nine-year-old children and several camp counselors. These are straight-forward, factual statements. The reality is brutal.

The roots of our American history are firmly planted in the hard reality of tragedy, loss, and disappointment, with sorrow handled traditionally through faith and perseverance. High hopes usually accompany our endeavors. This was the mindset when the Pilgrims left England. Knowing that nearly half of them died that first winter and spring, 1620–21, a reasonable reaction to this tragic fact is an incredulous, "But they came all this way with hopes and dreams and survived the hardships of the long ocean voyage. And then they died?" Heartbreak is a reality confirmed in the book of Job, *Yet man is born to trouble as the sparks fly upward* (Job 5:7 NKJV). But a broader life-truth is revealed in Ecclesiastes 3:1–8 NIV:

> *There is a time for everything,*
>   *and a season for every activity under the heavens:*
> 2 *a time to be born and a time to die,*
>   *a time to plant and a time to uproot,*
> 3 *a time to kill and a time to heal,*
>   *a time to tear down and a time to build,*
> 4 *a time to weep and a time to laugh,*
>   *a time to mourn and a time to dance,*
> 5 *a time to scatter stones and a time to gather them,*
>   *a time to embrace and a time to refrain from embracing,*
> 6 *a time to search and a time to give up,*
>   *a time to keep and a time to throw away,*
> 7 *a time to tear and a time to mend,*
>   *a time to be silent and a time to speak,*
> 8 *a time to love and a time to hate,*
>   *a time for war and a time for peace.*

My father-in-law, William Eugene Greenleaf, always penned his thoughts with simple yet profound prose. Three of his letters are included in *Letters: Our American Story* because they are a beautiful reflection on our common experience. It's an honor to include his writings, but he would be shocked to see his humble musings in print! The irony is that his son, Arie, in the early years of our marriage, occasionally threw his father's letters away, unopened, or after he'd scanned them for news only. He complained that faith was all his dad ever wrote about, and he wasn't interested. Oh, yes, how foolish and arrogant we can be. After his father died, Arie would come to wonderfully embrace and treasure those same words of faith.

The Greenleaf family has fascinating connections to American history, and Arie was able to acquire from his mother the most important book available to confirm his heritage: *A Genealogy of the Greenleaf Family*, by *Jonathan Greenleaf*, of Brooklyn, N.Y., 1854. Genealogical lines of descent are presented in *Group Charts*, beginning with the *Common Ancestor*, Edmund Greenleaf (ca.1600–1671). Even more intriguing, the author has included *Notes* that are detailed descriptions of some of the individuals and families listed.

Arie's fifth great-grandfather, *Honorable Johathan Greenleaf* (1723–1807), was born in Newbury, Massachusetts, and became a wealthy shipbuilder. He played a valuable role in the Revolutionary War, and, astoundingly, the description of his warmhearted personality in *Note 82* is the exact description of Arie's father, William Eugene, even to *the tones of his voice*:

> The stirring scenes of the Revolution engaged his energies. For the whole of that time he sustained some public office. He was a member of the Continental Congress at the commencement of the war, and after that in the Senate, the Council, or House of Representatives.
>
> His early advantages for education were limited, but he was a man of considerable reading, and had a large share of good common sense, joined with a good knowledge of human nature; and in addition to this, he possessed a remarkably kind and conciliating disposition. Even the tones of his voice were gentle and persuasive, and he was very frequently resorted to as a peacemaker between contending parties; and although he was not much of a speaker in public, yet he almost uniformly carried the point he had espoused.

Honorable Jonathan Greenleaf had a renowned grandson, Simon Greenleaf (1783–1853), and much is shared about him in *Note 89*. Simon was appointed "Royal Professor of Law" in 1833 at Harvard College in Cambridge. He succeeded U.S. Supreme Court Justice Joseph Story (1779–1845) as Dane Professor of Law at Harvard in 1846, an endowment position provided by Nathan Dane (1752–1835). Simon became professor emeritus when he retired to private life in 1848. His principal work is the *Treatise on the Law of Evidence* (3 vols, 1842–1853), which in its time was considered the most valuable resource on this topic. Harvard Law School established its excellence upon the scholarly work and teaching of professors Joseph Story and Simon Greenleaf.

... A Connecting Side Note: Connections occur between not only people but between cities, as well. Nathan Dane, a Massachusetts delegate to the Continental Congress, is called the "Father of American Jurisprudence." Dane County, Wisconsin, is named after him in honor of his work crafting the Northwest Ordinance (1787), which included his last-minute amendment banning slavery in the Northwest Territory. The largest city in Dane County is Madison, the state capital, and home to UW. It's a city of great importance to our family, not only educationally, but our daughter-in-law Dewa Shrestha Greenleaf grew up in Madison after coming from Kathmandu, Nepal, when she was four years old. Her mother came to pursue and receive her nursing degree from UW, and Dewa's dear parents still live there ...

Additional information in *Note 89* provides a deeper understanding of Simon's embrace of a strong Christian faith in his later years. His meticulous and renowned New Testament research, which was published in Boston in 1846 and reprinted a year later in London, is titled *An Examination of the Testimony of the Four Evangelists by the Rules of Evidence administered in Courts of Justice; with an account of the Trial of Jesus*. For many years, Simon was president of the Massachusetts Bible Society, and, astounding again, the description of his personality could be a description of William Eugene (they are first cousins four times removed), even to what they included in their correspondence:

> For the last thirty years of his life he was one of the most spiritually-minded men, evidently intent on walking humbly with God, and doing good to the bodies and souls of his fellow-men; scarce ever writing a letter of friendship even, without breathing in it a prayer, or delivering some gospel message.

Note 89 also shares a *sketch* that was published in *Cambridge Chronicle*, October 8, 1853, two days after Simon died, defining his academic and literary success. The description of his teaching style could apply to a son I know, Dr. Arie Todd Greenleaf (first cousin to Simon, six times removed), making genetic heritage, again, a marvel to contemplate:

> As an instructor he was greatly beloved, and his lectures and teachings were clear, distinct, and practical. As a counselor he was clear, safe, and practical. His advice was always characterized by a weight of common sense as well as legal skill, which was sufficient to secure confidence while it gave direction.

One other mention about the Greenleaf family is their connection to the famous American poet, John Greenleaf Whittier (1807–1892). Their common ancestor is Edmund, making Whittier my husband's first cousin nine times removed. This family history is shared as an incentive for others to pursue knowledge about their families, an encouragement to "look at you" and be amazed by the strength, courage, and efforts of your ancestors and all they accomplished, despite any obstacle.

Challenges surprise us. Disasters are rarely anticipated. The cataclysmic destruction from Hurricane Helene (2024), the Guadalupe River flooding (2025), and the Los Angeles Palisades fire (2025) are forever heartbreaking. In the face of tragedy, a deep well of strength is needed to keep going. This is also true for every creative attempt that gets thwarted, in whatever realm the effort is made. It's daunting to lose what one has worked hard to create. Jonathan Greenleaf, the author of *A Genealogy of the Greenleaf Family*, included a Preface with a paragraph that took my breath away in contemplating the literary loss and then courage it took to accomplish his genealogical treasure. His determination is inspiring:

> There has been an unavoidable delay in the publication, owing to the fact that at one of the severe fires in New York, during the past winter, nearly one half of the copy, then in the printer's hands, and partly in type, was entirely destroyed, and the loss has been with difficulty supplied; and should any confusion appear in the arrangement, it may be attributed to this.
>
> The author will thankfully receive any corrections which can be made, and any additional information which may be given, intending to preserve and record everything of the kind for the benefit of posterity, should it ever be needed.
> JONATHAN GREENLEAF
> Brooklyn, N.Y., April, 1854

Letter – William Eugene Greenleaf, 1972

10–25–72
7:20 a.m.

Dear Ann and Arie:

We received six letters in one day from our children and mothers. One also came from sister Martha. It took me nearly an hour to read them all.

Perhaps I could read them in less time but I like to read between the lines also.

Being the creatures that we are, many times we leave more information between the lines than in the lines.

And sometimes what we didn't say speaks louder than what we did say.

To say the least, I am glad you have purchased a house and will soon be in it.

This change will afford you many changes, challenges, readjustments, trials, victories.

And the love you have for each other will be your sunshine in the dark.

Your warmth when things seem cold.

Your happiness when things could have been sad.

Your confidence and determination in the future in the face of so many odds.

And three finer ones never have I met.

I am very proud of you and your family.

And may the God of our fathers bring you constant Peace.

And may Grace be with you three,

Our Lord Jesus Christ.

Your father & Grandfather,

Eugene

NOVEMBER

CHAPTER 23 ... THE GIFT OF ENCOURAGEMENT

My Connection to Elisabeth Elliot
Postcard: Elisabeth Elliot Gren, 1998
"Thank You Note" Excerpt: Valerie Elliot Shepard, 2025

Chapter 23

The Gift of Encouragement

My Connection to Elisabeth Elliot
This 1998 postcard message is Elisabeth's heartfelt thank you for the *encouraging words* in my letter explaining how much her books meant to me.

RESIDING WITHIN THE "CAN DO" American spirit of inner strength, courage, and determination is a bit of its English ancestry. The ethos of Great Britain is that classic expression "Keep Calm and Carry On." It was created by Britain's Ministry of Information in 1939, one of three messages to encourage its country at the start of World War II. The phrase was unused, and posters were discarded, until one was discovered tucked away in a Northumberland bookstore in 2000, and the exhortation became ubiquitous. It is a principle that bolsters resilience in the face of adversity and makes "can do" possible.

Most of us are drawn to stories of perseverance, and how people go forward despite hardships and loss. Reality Television with its adventure programing of individuals overcoming challenges is no accident, as in the success of *American Ninja Warrior*. We admire gumption in the face of difficult odds, or in the way people handle creepy things, such as eating worms and scorpions, brains and all animal parts, ala the television program *Alone*, another favorite. In that program, we contemplate our responses and how we would do things differently, perhaps, or if we could even do them at all, which is my thought, as people munch on questionable things to get much-needed fat and protein into their spare diet.

Tales of adversity handled by grace make meaningful testimonies of faith. Elisabeth Howard Elliot (1926–2015), Christian missionary, author, lecturer, and syndicated radio host is one of those individuals who has inspired many with her life story and that of her first husband, Jim Elliot (1927–1956). Wisdom shared from her experiences and truth from the Bible, offered with an honest, humble awareness of human need, are the themes of her forty-eight books (of which I have twelve), her speaking engagements, and her radio programs. Listening to *Gateway to Joy* on the radio day after day for thirteen years made an indelible impression and was a great encouragement and help. God's love was the foundation of Elisabeth's daily message, based on the truth of a powerful verse. *The eternal God is your refuge, and underneath are the everlasting arms* (Deuteronomy 33:27 NKJV).

Elisabeth Elliot's fourteenth book, *These Strange Ashes* (Servant Publications 1998, Harper & Row 1975), especially speaks to the interplay of faith, trust, and God's will and is a favorite of mine. Her South American mission adventure takes place in Santo Domingo de los Colorados in the western foothills of the Andes Mountains of Ecuador, the year prior to marrying Jim in 1953. While she was there, he was doing mission work in Shandia in the rain forest of eastern Ecuador. Even Elisabeth in her Preface states, *I confess to feeling a certain tenderness for this book. It tells the story of my earliest lessons in the sovereignty of God—three stunning ones, assigned to me in the first year as a jungle missionary* (Elliot, *These Strange Ashes*, 9).

With humor and relatable emotion, she describes the difficulties living in a primitive environment while attempting *to translate the Bible for the Colorado Indians* (Elliot, *These Strange Ashes*, 50), who only had an oral language. Elisabeth, as well as Jim, had taken the Summer Institute of Linguistics presented by the Wycliffe Bible Translators at the University of Oklahoma, and she was eager to implement what she learned. Her greatest work-related need was finding the very essential *informant*, the person who would help with the language translation. When no one was immediately forthcoming, Elisabeth embraced a vividly descriptive verse which she quoted many times throughout her ministry. The Scripture's encouragement reiterates God's promise of help in our time of need and gives voice to our determination to stay faithful and carry on. *For the Lord God will help me; therefore shall I not be confounded: therefore have I set my face like a flint, and I know that I shall not be ashamed* (Isaiah 50:7 KJV).

One of the most riveting tales of sacrifice, adventure, and faith is found in Elisabeth's first book, *Through Gates of Splendor* (Tyndale House 1981, 1957, 1956). It is the true story of the five young missionary families who attempt contact with the Waorani (Huaorani) tribe, an indigenous and isolated people group who reside between the Curaray and Napo Rivers in the Amazon jungle of eastern Ecuador. They were also called the "Auca," meaning "savage" in the Quechua language, for their hostile, life-ending interactions with anyone who entered their territory, and for the revenge killings within their tribe. The five missionary families are Jim Elliot (Elisabeth), Pete Fleming (Olive), Ed McCully (Marilou), Nate Saint (Marj), and Roger Youderian (Barbara).

The mission movement in America (with historic roots in Great Britain and Europe) is established on verses in the Bible which inspire individuals and families to serve as missionaries in their home country or abroad. They accept the call on their hearts to share the eternal, life-giving salvation message of faith in Jesus Christ, as defined in three key passages in Scripture:

> The Gospel Message
> *For God so loved the world that He gave His only begotten Son,*
> *that whoever believes in Him should not perish but have*
> *everlasting life.*
> John 3:16 NKJV

> The Great Commission
> *And Jesus came and spake unto them, saying,*
> *All power is given unto me in heaven and in earth.*
> *Go ye therefore and teach all nations, baptizing them*
> *in the name of Father, and of the Son, and of the Holy Ghost:*
> *Teaching them to observe all things whatsoever I have*
> *commanded you:*
> *and, lo, I am with you always, even until the end of the world. Amen.*
> Matthew 28:18–20 KJV

> *And [Jesus] said to them,*
> *"Go into all the world and preach the gospel to every creature."*
> Mark 16:15 NKJV

NOVEMBER

After they married, Jim and Elisabeth served in Shell Mera in eastern Ecuador as missionaries to the Quichua Indians, where their daughter, Valerie, was born in 1955. Stories about the fierceness of the Auca Indians, who were located not far from their home station, intensified their desire to reach them. Four other families joined them in an outreach called "Operation Auca," their effort to establish a relationship with the Waorani to ultimately share the gospel message of John 3:16. For several months, beginning in October 1955, Mission Aviation Fellowship (MAF) pilot, Nate Saint, dropped pictures and presents from his bright yellow Piper Cruiser, using a bucket-drop system he developed, and the Waorani responded with their own gifts. Dayuma, a Waorani woman who had escaped the village when her father and relatives were killed, helped Jim acquire a vocabulary to interact with the Auca. Every contact was an attempt to mitigate danger, and confidence grew through the positive interactions from the air. In early January 1956, the five men established a camp on a sandbar on the Curaray River they named "Palm Beach," and two Waorani women and a young man visited them in a long and friendly encounter. Then on January 8, five days after setting up camp, their lives were taken when they were speared and killed by six Auca tribesmen. Their deaths became international news titled the "Auca Incident," and *Life* magazine did an intensive, ten-page photojournalist (Cornell Capa) article that shocked the world titled "'Go Ye and Preach the Gospel' Five Do and Die" (Jan. 30, 1956).

Two more riveting accounts were written by Elisabeth concerning this tragedy and the years following. They are *Shadow of the Almighty: The Life and Testament of Jim Elliot* (Harper Collins 1989, 1979, 1958) and *The Savage My Kinsman* (Servant Publications 1981, Harper 1961), which is a remarkable telling of an opportunity given to Elisabeth and Rachel Saint (sister of pilot Nate Saint) to reside with the Waorani. These two women were asked to return to the Auca settlement and live, which they successfully did, sharing forgiveness, love, and the faith that redeems. Elisabeth and Valerie left after several years with a full life ahead for Elisabeth with remarriage (twice) and a far-reaching literary and speaking career. Valerie married Rev. Walter Shepard Jr., and they are the parents of eight children. They were active in ministry for over forty-five years until his retirement. The Shepards pastored several churches and were missionaries in the Democratic Republic of Congo (2005–2008). Valerie is the author of *Devotedly: The Personal Letters and Love Story of Jim and Elisabeth Elliot* (B&H Books

2019), and *Pilipinto: The Jungle Adventures of a Missionary's Daughter* (P&R Publishing 2023).

Rachel Saint (1914–1994) spent the rest of her life working with the "Waodani," as the Waorani are called today, a term meaning "the people." Steve Saint (1951), son of Nate and Marj Saint, published a memoir, *End of the Spear: A True Story* (Saltriver 2005), which was made into a movie in 2006. Each surviving widow and her children went on to experience fulfilling and meaningful lives of faith.

The whole of our American story is impossible to tell, because the whole is comprised of everyone's individual story, which is a vast and complex unfolding of events, circumstances, emotions, and genetic influence. The writings of Elisabeth Elliot are deeply impactful and compelling and speak to us in every situation. They provide insight into the commonality of our human struggles. She explores the same questions, doubts, and fears we all face, and her faithful determination to trust God, no matter what, is an encouragement for all of us. Elisabeth cherished the author and Christian missionary from County Down, Ireland, Amy Carmichael (1867–1951), who served in India for fifty-five years. Elisabeth embraced Carmichael's simple but profound message, "In acceptance lieth peace" (Henderson, "Living with a Legacy," 2022).

Our thoughts, both written and spoken; our efforts, both grand and modest; and our prayers, both thankful and desperate, have an arch of impact that is rarely understood. They weren't expressed in a vacuum but instead exist and compound beyond the moment. Their future influence and fulfillment are a mystery wrapped in Divine sovereignty that plays out in people's lives in unexpected ways. Elisabeth's first several books opened a floodgate of American missionary adventure and commitment that is ongoing, despite her honest portrayal of the hardships that accompany mission work: the loneliness, self-doubt, and losses. But clearly, joys are also part of the story, with the underlying issue one of faith and trust in God. When Elisabeth shared her husband's story, she gave the world a statement Jim Elliot penned in his journal in 1949 (*Shadow of the Almighty*, 247), a succinct and impactful definition of the sacrifice given in mission work, a statement that reflects the essence of our life as believers and followers of Jesus Christ.

> He is no fool who gives what he cannot keep
> to gain what he cannot lose.
> Jim Elliot

Postcard ~ Elisabeth Elliot, 1998

ELISABETH ELLIOT GREN—STRAWBERRY COVE— MAGNOLIA, MASSACHUSETTS

November 27, 1998

Dear Ann,

Thank you so much, dear Ann, for your encouraging words of November 15. It's always heartening to know that someone has not only read some of my books, but has actually reread some of them.

Do please squeeze me into your prayers if God, from time to time, brings my name to mind. I do need the constant anointing and correcting from my heavenly Father that I may be a faithful carrier of His word and example in my own life. Pray that I may be faithful where nobody's looking.

Gratefully,
Elisabeth

It's impossible to read anything Elisabeth writes and not feel the challenge personally. Her self-evaluation and continuous seeking of God's will to be a faithful witness of his mercy and goodness, privately and publicly, inspire me to do the same.

I received a lovely thoughtfulness from Elisabeth's daughter, Valerie, and the power of encouragement continues. The importance of encouraging others is one of the most important conclusions to be understood from *Letters: Our American Story*. Like mother, like daughter:

THANK YOU EXCERPT ~ VALERIE ELLIOT SHEPARD, 2025

June 23, 2025
Dear Ann—
May the Lord <u>bless</u> your work and fill your heart with joy!
Sincerely,
Valerie

DECEMBER

CHAPTER 24 ... BUILDING MEMORIES

My Connection to Carolyn Greenleaf Potterville and Laurie Opperman Greenleaf
Letter: Carolyn Greenleaf Potterville, 2018
Letter: Laurie Opperman Greenleaf, 1979

CHAPTER 25 ... GRANDCHILDREN, OUR JOY

My Connection to Divya and Aarush Greenleaf
Text Messages: Aarush Greenleaf, 2024
Letter and Poem: Divya Greenleaf, 2024

LETTER CLOSINGS ... A BENEDICTION

My Connection to Donald and Arthena Wray Brubaker, Joe and Lorraine Eller Brubaker, LaDrue and Irene Turner Wray
Letter Closings: Kansas Second Cousins, 2001–2008

HOW THIS BOOK WAS ACCOMPLISHED

Chapter 24

Building Memories

*My Connection to Carolyn Greenleaf Potterville
and Laurie Opperman Greenleaf
These two letters span thirty-nine years and offer a chance to 'relive' a
special day, with the intervening years ones for building memories
for old age.*

OUR AMERICAN TALE EXPANDS through the uniting of families through marriage, and sisters-in-law can hold a special place in the story. Laurie, Ginny, and I married into the Greenleaf family (husbands are the brothers Daniel, Bill, and Arie). We became sisters-in-law to each other and to Carolyn (Butch Potterville) and Mary Margaret (Ken Palmer). A loving connection has existed from the start.

Carol and Butch lived the farthest away in Alaska, moving to South Dakota in 2004, yet they always made the effort to visit family in Peoria, Illinois. Sometimes they'd drive up to Northern Wisconsin afterward to visit Arie and me before we moved south in 2002. Carol had an abiding commitment to her siblings, and she was truly a light that shone brightly upon the family. When Arie was diagnosed with cancer in August 2003, his family rallied around him with cards, telephone calls, and gifts. Carol's crocheted lap-robe, deep blue with rows of burgundy and pale blue arrived at the hospital for Arie's first, five-day cancer treatment. It's still on my loveseat. Cancer's fearful blow was softened through the kindness of family and friends. This is the American Way. We are family to each other through our emotional support and efforts, the food we bring in time of need, and the prayers we lift for comfort, healing, and strength.

As treatments ran their course, and Hospice was the next step in this journey, the time came for admittance to the Elizabeth House. This Hospice home was the peaceful and caring environment we needed for Arie's last twelve days. Carol and Butch were in the process of moving and couldn't fly to North Carolina, but the rest of Arie's family came to see him for a final good-bye. Mary Margaret left immediately and drove from East Peoria to be with us and take care of our home and our two cats while I stayed with Arie at the Elizabeth House. What an enormous blessing she was, beyond any expectation. Singing beloved hymns provided a sweet peace for Arie, and the first time Mary joined me, it was a thrill to discover how similar our voices were. We had so much fun singing together, we sang one of our favorite songs at Arie's memorial service, "What a Day That Will Be" (James Hill, 1955). When the emotion of the moment took over, Mary was able to finish singing the hymn's inspiring, hopeful message. How grateful I was for her presence. As a parting gift, she gave me a lamb stuffie, the first of my collection, because we are sheep who belong to the Good Shepard. This is especially true when traversing the "valley" described in Psalm 23 NKJV:

> *The Lord is my shepherd;*
> *I shall not want.*
> *2 He makes me to lie down in green pastures;*
> *He leads me beside the still waters.*
> *3 He restores my soul;*
> *He leads me in the paths of righteousness*
> *For His name's sake.*
> *4 Yea, though I walk through the valley of the shadow of death,*
> *I will fear no evil;*
> *For You are with me;*
> *Your rod and Your staff, they comfort me.*
> *5 You prepare a table before me in the presence of my enemies;*
> *You anoint my head with oil;*
> *My cup runs over.*
> *6 Surely goodness and mercy shall follow me*
> *All the days of my life;*
> *And I will dwell in the house of the Lord*
> *Forever.*

Our needs are great and varied, from sickness, to job concerns, to personal loss. Sensitive support soothes the burdens we carry. Carol's compassion for her family lifted many a load, something we all experienced. Her 2018 response to a letter her sister-in-law, Laurie, had written, is a reminder of how important it is to appreciate life and treat others with a spirit of kindness and generosity. Carol tucked Laurie's 1979 letter and recipe away, and it was found thirty-nine years later in a recipe book. This is a marvelous demonstration of the arch that carries an action or event forward in time to a moment of revealing.

Laurie's letter is a sweet telling of everyday life in December, even though her husband's job was on hold because of a strike at the world-famous Caterpillar Tractor Company, where he was employed. Much was unknown: how long would the strike last, and when would Dan resume work and receive a paycheck? They had an almost two-year old daughter, Amy, and a baby was due in the spring. There were many concerns, but the excitement and preparations for Christmas could not be contained. These two letters offer a relatable and inspiring glimpse into dear people who exemplify the blessings that come from choosing joy and thankfulness amid life's uncertainties:

> A joyful heart is good medicine,
> but a crushed spirit dries up the bones.
> Proverbs 17:22 ESV

Letter ~ Carolyn Greenleaf Potterville, 2018

Jan. 23, 2018

Laurie, Laurie!

    In looking in the Betty Crocker Cookbook (which I VERY seldom ever use), I discovered wrapped around an oatmeal cookie recipe you sent . . . this delightful letter from you. As much as I enjoy reading it, I think it might bring you greater Joy to have it . . . kind of a way to "relive" a special day in your life.

    You and Dan were in the prime of youth, dreams, & challenges. Of course, ole Carolyn was off in Alaska building memories for my "old age" and missed this special time in your lives.

    Don't suppose this money will take you on much of a date, but it <u>may</u> cover the popcorn for a home movie. Ha.

    Love to You & Dan
    Carolyn

Letter ~ Laurie Opperman Greenleaf, 1979

December 14, 1979

Dear Carolyn,

I'm finally getting a recipe to you that you asked for almost a year ago. I feel terrible that I've put this off so long.

I've been so busy this week with baking, crocheting gifts, putting up the tree and decorations, shopping and studying for my bible class which is tonight. I feel like I need at least one more week plus what we have till Christmas.

Dan has been on strike since October, so I don't get quite as much done now that he is home all the time because he needs attention too. It's been fun having him around more but then we haven't been able to go out much either because of no money. Anyway we've been getting by.

Amy enjoyed seeing the tree all lit up. You should have heard her oohs and ahs. She's so cute when she does that.

We were over at Mary Margaret's house last week and couldn't believe how big Nathan had got. [He was ten months old, their fourth and last child after Philip, Susan, and Darren.] He weighs as much as Amy, around 22 lbs. He has really got an appetite. Amy on the other hand is finicky.

Our next baby is due [the end of March] and Amy's birthday is [soon after]. It seems like I'm getting bigger faster with this one.

We think it will be a boy. Time will tell. [It was a boy, their son Joe, and son Bill came several years later].

Write us when you get a chance. Dan sends his love.
Love,
Laurie

Chapter 25

Grandchildren, Our Joy

My Connection to Divya and Aarush Greenleaf
These text messages from my grandson, simple yet deeply meaningful, and this Christmas letter and poem from my granddaughter, astonishingly insightful, convey their love *and are treasures to their* Grammy's *heart.*

WHEN OUR SON, ARIE Todd, was born, his Grandfather Greenleaf expressed his joy and prayers in a letter shared in Chapter 22. The juxtaposition of adding his words in this book, *love, good wishes, concern, hopes for Todd's future*, and where his grandson was at that moment is a powerful revealing of the arch of life. My son was in Barcelona, Spain, speaking at The Science of Consciousness Conference, July 6–11, 2025, something that would have thrilled, astounded, and brought great pride to both his grandfather and father, as it does to Patrick and me.

William Eugene Greenleaf penned another life truth about the birth of his grandson; *I can't explain to you my feeling exactly. So you will have to wait a few years until you are Grandparents.* He was right, a grandparent's feelings are indescribable, especially when their grandchildren convey their love. Aarush's dear comments, written when he was twelve years old, came via texting, the modern-day vehicle of communication. His messages convey a connection that means everything to me:

> Thank you so much for the card grammy!
> Have an amazing easter
> Yay! Can't wait to see you
> I hope the book your writing does well!
> I can't wait to see you at my birthday!
> I'm glad your coming to visit me
> I love you and miss you so much

As Aarush's sweet messages are dear to my heart, so are Divya's 2024 Christmas letter and poem, written when she was fourteen. We had driven to Florida to celebrate the holiday, and while just being together was enough, receiving her special note and creative expression was not anticipated and brought that inexpressible grandparent joy. In her letter, Divya mentions the poem I had written for her birthday, "Our Stuffies," an ode to our mutual love for stuffed animals. It begins:

> Irresistible they are,
> Our stuffies, or "plushies,"
> My granddaughter calls them,
> Girl with a heart like mine,
> Our stuffed animals that bring
> A smile, peering from bookcase,
> From basket, from bed
> Lined in a row, comforting,
> Adorable, great for a cuddle,
> Even a kiss, lifting our spirits
> And easing our thoughts which
> Whirl with life ever tugging us
> This way and that.

It was gratifying and humbling to learn my literary musing was inspirational and led to the very enthralling poem she wrote and titled "The Final Duet for Ill-fated Lovers." Divya's nine years of ballet and then figure skating are reflected in her rhythmic descriptions. Even more compelling and astounding, though, is her mature sensitivity to human emotion and interaction, making her intuitive poem remarkable for her age.

Divya's talent is no surprise, for there are famous poets now and centuries ago found in both lines of her paternal ancestry. John Greenleaf Whittier is a distant first cousin, and award-winning American-born,

English poet and playwright, T.S. Eliot (born in St. Louis, Missouri, 1888–died in London, England, 1965) is also a cousin. Eliot won the Nobel Prize in Literature (1948) *for his outstanding, pioneering contribution to present-day poetry.* He was a leader in the Modernist Movement which confronted and poetically interpreted modern society and its complexities. His Great-Great-Grandmother is Elizabeth Greenleaf (1781–1853), a descendant of Edmund Greenleaf.

On my side is the poet Francis Quarles (1592–1644) of Romford, Essex, England, who is Divya's eleventh great-grandfather. He is a well-known religious and Metaphysical poet who united emotion with intellectual observation. His most famous work is *Emblems* (1635), a combination of poetry and detailed, moralistic imagery addressing issues of faith and the virtues needed to handle life's struggles. Our relationship with Francis Quarles brings the whole of this book full circle. Francis married Ursula Woodgate (1602–1646), and they had eighteen children. Our family descends from their daughter Joanna (1630–1682). The "Ursula" name shows up many times in later generations, a common practice. Great-Grandmother Mary Ursula Kessler Vandivert, who was introduced in the first chapter, is named for her grandmother Ursula Smith Alvord, each a descendant of Ursula Woodgate Quarles.

A final sharing reveals the wonder of genealogy, our racial heritage, and our personal interconnectedness. Langston Hughes (1901–1967), the revered poet, novelist, playwright, and social activist known as the leader of the Harlem Renaissance, an African American cultural and political movement in the 1920s and '30s, is also a descendant of the Quarles family. Hughes gives a fascinating account about his multi-racial ancestry, available on *Kansas History Web Sites*. He writes, *There are lots of different kinds of blood in our family*, and then identifies his African American, English, Scottish, and Cherokee Indian roots. He makes a surprising reference to Clark County, Kentucky. His grandmother's father on his paternal side, Silas Cushenberry, lived there in 1850 (WikiTree) as *a Jewish slave trader*, and was the one who contributed *the white blood* in his father's family. He is also related to famous Kentucky lawyer and statesman Henry Clay (1777–1852). Hughes then explains his connection with the Quarles family:

> On my mother's side, I had a paternal great-grandfather named Quarles—Captain Ralph Quarles—who was white and lived in Louisa County, Virginia, before the Civil War, and who had several colored children by a colored housekeeper, who was his slave.

The Quarles traced their ancestry back to Francis Quarles, famous Jacobean poet, who wrote, "A Feast for Wormes."

... A Literary Sidenote: Quarles poem, "A Feast for Wormes" (1620), is based on *Jonah* from the Bible. He presents the sincere response of the Ninevites to Jonah's call for repentance. He compares their genuine sorrow with disingenuous faith, a reflection of the Puritan mindset which sought the same sincerity of faith and brought the Pilgrims here that same year ...

Genealogical records for Langston Hughes and the Quarles family indicate Hughes is our very distant cousin through Sir Francis Robert Quarles (1508–1585) who had two lines of descent through two different wives. The first line leads through son George (1528–1585) to Langston Hughes, and the second line is through son James (1557–1599) to Francis Quarles, then to our family and to millions of others. My best understanding, subject to error, is Hughes and Quarles are first cousins ten times removed.

According to Dr. Henry Louis Gates Jr. in a PBS interview with host Terry Gross, recorded earlier and presented on his program *Fresh Air* on January 21, 2019, *the average African American is 24 percent European* ... [The test to determine this] *is called an admixture test ... which measures your ancestry back 500 years.* It is exciting to discover one's genetic heritage, which I did through *Ancestry,* though other companies are available. The *Ancestry* DNA test is easy to accomplish and usually confirms what we know about our family through the study of genealogy, but there are surprises. The ancestral breakdown from each parent is determined, which is always fascinating. One's *Ancestral Regions* are also identified, which in my case is primarily England and Northwestern Europe, with Scotland and Germanic Europe in the mix.

As a nation, we plainly connect with each other. *Letters: Our American Story* demonstrates this reality through a combination of history, genealogy, and faith. This book is presented to say, "Look at your family and see the vastness of your own remarkable story and how we fit together!" As this mission winds down, the initial desire to share my father's WWII letter concludes with his great-grandchildren's writings, an epistolary journey which has included many letters, all portraying our common American experience and connection. The heart of each author has been expressed in the relatable circumstances, events, struggles, and joys they penned, an encouragement to learn, embrace, and cherish your own family's story, for it is part of the fabric that makes up America's 250th Anniversary.

Letter and Poem ~ Divya Greenleaf, 2024

Merry Christmas Grammy! I'm so grateful to spend this Christmas with you. (heart) I love you so much. You're the best grandmother ever and I wouldn't trade you for the world haha. (heart) [Divya's Nepali grandmother is her "Bajai," and her grandfather is "Baje," and they are the best Nepali grandparents ever.] You're a very special person Grammy and everyone is blessed to know you. I love your poetry so so much, the adorable poem you wrote me for my birthday has got to be one of my favorites haha. (heart) I've been starting to take up poetry recently so I wanted to share one of my poems with you! This one is titled:

THE FINAL DUET FOR ILL-FATED LOVERS

I don't know how to dance,
My clumsy steps, your elegant stance,
A duet for ill-fated lovers,
Breaking apart in the arms of each other.

A duet can't be easy with someone unknowing,
Your heart stepped aside and you left my heart growing.
I stumbled through the words left unsaid,
Your movements were graceful but expression screamed dread.

I knew our embrace was sure to diminish,
Each step out of place, each turn left unfinished.
Your rhythm, a melody I couldn't attain,
My faltering feet met with silent disdain.

The music, once vibrant, grew heavy with sorrow,
Each note a reminder of no shared tomorrow.
You waltzed with precision, I stumbled, I fell,
But in that last moment, the silence did tell.

I saw in your eyes both regret and a tear,
A love out of time, yet achingly clear.

Love you, Grammy, Merry Christmas!

Letter Closings

A Benediction

My Connection to Kansas Second Cousins
Donald and Arthena Wray Brubaker, Joe and Lorraine Eller Brubaker,
LaDrue and Irene Turner Wray
As a correspondence concludes with a closing, this book ends with exquisitely penned blessings received as a benediction from my Kansas cousins.

(December 2001)
The season of Christmas brings loved ones so near—
<u>new</u> <u>friends</u> and old friends, those we hold dear—
We are remembering you with Love and Prayers.
God bless you both dearly—
Donald and Arthena B.

(Christmas 2002)
The gift God gave to us is Jesus Christ His Son,
worthy of our life and love—
given for everyone.
Donald and Arthena

(Thanksgiving 2004)
God Loves You, so do we—
Lovingly,
Your Cousins,
Donald and Arthena

(Christmas 2005)
May you have the gift of faith,
the blessing of hope,
and the peace of His love
at Christmas and always—
Lovingly,
Joe & Lorraine

(Christmas 2005)
We send all of you our deepest wishes for a God-filled season,
and His love in the New Year 2006.
Love and blessings,
LaDrue, Irene, Dana

(September Birthday 2005)
God bless you
with His good care
and a happy day!
Donald and Arthena B.

(Christmas 2008)
We pray the blessings of Christ
and the joy of family and friends
are blended together with the peace of God
for your Christmas—
Love You Two,
Donald and Arthena

Till we meet again . . .

How This Book Was Accomplished

"This is the word of the Lord to Zerubbabel:
'Not by might nor by power, but by My Spirit,'
Says the Lord of hosts.
7 'Who are you, O great mountain?
Before Zerubbabel you shall become a plain!
And he shall bring forth the capstone
With shouts of "Grace, grace to it!" ' "
Zechariah 4:6–7 NKJV

Thank You!
I'm grateful you have read my book.
May the message of historical accomplishment, individual achievement, and faith be a blessing and an inspiration to understand your own place in American history.

If *Letters: Our American Story* has been meaningful, please consider posting a review on www.Amazon.com. This ensures others will find and enjoy our national story.
Thank You!

Bibliography

Adelman, Garry, et al. "A House Divided: Civil War Kentucky." *Hallowed Ground Magazine* (December 21, 2021).

The Age of Aquarius. "Medley: Aquarius/Let the Sunshine In." The 5th Dimension. Soul City, 1969. https://en.wikipedia.org/wiki/Aquarius/Let_the_Sunshine_In.

All Poetry. *From 'A Feast for Wormes."* Franceis Quarles. https://allpoetry.com/poem/14374041-From—A-Feast-For-Wormes—by-Francis-Quarles.

American War Memorials Overseas. *20th Armored Division Dachau Liberation Plaque.* https://www.uswarmemorials.org/html/monument_details.php?SiteID=67&MemID=120.

Ammann, Jakob. "Ammann, Jakob (17th/18th Century)" Global Anabaptist Mennonite Encyclopedia. https://gameo.org/index.php?title=Ammann,_Jakob_(17th/18th_century).

Ancestry.com. "World's Largest Genealogy Site." Ancestry.com®.

Ancestry of Mary (Perkins) Bradbury. FamousKin.com. https://famouskin.com/family-tree.php?name=3419+mary+bradbury.

Anthony, Susan B. The Dobkin Family Collection of Feminism. New York. https://www.dobkinfeminism.org/sponsored-research/.

Apollo 11 Mission Overview. NASA. https://www.nasa.gov/history/apollo-11-mission-overview/.

Austin, Charles. "Obituary; Catherine Marshall, 68, Author" (March 19, 1983). https://www.nytimes.com/1983/03/19/obituaries/obituary-catherine-marshall-68-author.html.

"Auca" Incident Collection. Identifier: CN 599. Evangelism & Missions Archives. Wheaton College. https://archives.wheaton.edu/repositories/4/resources/278.

Berry, Melissa. "The Witchcraft Trial of Mary Perkins Bradbury." *Genealogy Magazine.com,* 2015. https://www.genealogymagazine.com/witchcraft-trial/.

Blumberg, Jess. "A Brief History of the Salem Witch Trials." *Smithsonian Magazine* (October 24, 2022). https://www.smithsonianmag.com/history/a-brief-history-of-the-salem-witch-trials-175162489/.

Bing, Elisabeth, R.P.T. *Six Practical Lessons for an Easier Childbirth.* New York: Bantam Books, 1967.

Birbriar, Lana. "How Nathan Dane finally got to Wisconsin." Origin Story. *Harvard Law Bulletin* (November 24, 2014) https://hls.harvard.edu/today/origin-story/.

BIBLIOGRAPHY

Bradley Polytechnic Institute *Bradley Polytechnic Institute: the first decade*, 1897–1907. Peoria, Illinois (1908) 106, 145. https://archive.org/details/bradleypolytech noobraduoft/page/144/mode/2up.

Bradley University Library. *The Tech*. Nov (1899) 18; *The Tech*. Christmas (1899) 8–9. https://archive.org/details/bradleyuniversitylibrary. https://archive.org/details/tech 1899-1900/V3N1_November%201899/.

Bright, Sarah Guthrie. *Normal Schools / Definition, Training & History*. Study.com, (updated Nov. 21, 2023). https://study.com/academy/lesson/normal-schools-in-america-role-in-teacherpreparation.html.

Brown, Janice. "The Remick Family & Museum of Tamworth, New Hampshire." Cow Hampshire Blog (January 21, 2007). https://www.cowhampshireblog.com/2007 /01/21/the-remick-family-museum-of-tamworth-new-hampshire/.

Brubaker, Marwin E., and Margaret Brubaker Eller. *Descendants of John and Anna Myers Brubaker,* 1750–1995. Morgantown, Pennsylvania: Masthof, 1996.

Caleb Johnson's Mayflower History.com. "Richard Warren." https://mayflowerhistory. com/warren/.

College Symposium of the Kansas State Agricultural College. Manhattan, Kansas. The Hall & O'Donald Litho (1891) 61, 62, 79, 107.

Combs, Josiah H. "Combs, a Study in Comparative Philology and Genealogy." Norris K. Combs. Pensacola, Florida, 1976. Electronically reprinted by the Combs & Research Group in 1999. https://combs-families.org/combs/jhc/ms-jhc.html.

Cox, Savannah. "A Brief History of the Hippies, The 1960s Movement That Changed America" (April 4, 2013; Updated November 7, 2023). https://allthatsinteresting. com/a-brief-history-of-hippies.

The Elisabeth Elliot Foundation. "About Elisabeth Elliot." https://elisabethelliot.org/ about/.

———. "About Valerie Elliot Shepard." https://elisabethelliot.org/about/valerie-elliot-shepard/.

Elliot, Elisabeth. *Through Gates of Splendor*. Wheaton: Tyndale House (1981, 1956).

———. *Shadow of the Almighty*. San Francisco: Harper Collins (1989, 1958) 247.

———. *These Strange Ashes*. Ann Arbor: Servant Publications (1998, 1975) 9, 50.

———. *The Savage My Kinsman*. Ann Arbor: Servant Publications (1989, 1961).

Fisher, Julie. "Peter Folger and Up-Biblum" APS Library (December 11, 2018). https:// www.amphilsoc.org/blog/peter-folger-and-biblum.

Freeland, Gloria. "Riley County History–Annie Pillsbury: Manhattan postmaster, writer and activist." *The Mercury* (May 24, 2020) https://themercury.com/news/ riley-county-history-annie-pillsbury-manhattan-postmaster-writer-and-activist/ article_19e95868-f2b9-5885-a388-eldb32e7a6fl.html.

Garber, Steve. NASA. "Sputnik and The Dawn of the Space Age" (Oct. 10, 2007). https:// www.nasa.gov/history/sputnik/index.html.

Gates, Henry Louis. "Historian Henry Louis Gates Jr. On DNA Testing and Finding His Own Roots." Terry Gross. PBS. Heard on *Fresh Air*, January 21, 2019. https://www. npr.org/2019/01/21/686531998/historian-henry-louis-gates-jr-on-dna-testing-and-finding-his-own-roots.

The German Baptist Church. "The History of the Early Church." https://earlychurch.com/ german-baptist-brethren/.

Greenleaf, Arie T. "The Dynamis Theory Unveiled:" The Science of Consciousness Conf. Barcelona, July 6–11, 2025.

Greenleaf, Jonathan. *A Genealogy of the Greenleaf Family*. New York: Edward O. Jenkins, 1854.

Greenleaf, Simon. Encyclopedia.com: Columbia University. 6th ed. https://www.encyclopedia.com/reference/encyclopedias-almanacs-transcripts-and-maps/greenleaf-simon.

Hayward, Nancy. "Susan B. Anthony (1820–1906)" The National Women's History Museum (2018) https://www.womenshistory.org/education-resources/biographies/susan-b-anthony.

Henderson, Kim. "Living with a legacy." *World Magazine* (August 11, 2022). https://wng.org/articles/living-with-a-legacy-1659845584.

Hickam, Homer H. Jr. *Rocket Boys*. New York: Delacorte, 1998. *October Sky*. Reprinted, New York: Dell, 1999.

"Historical Essay. Jones, Nellie Kedzie 1858–1956." Wisconsin Historical Society. https://www.wisconsinhistory.org/Records/Article/CS521.

History.com Editors. "19th Century Westward Expansion." https://www.history.com/articles/westward-expansion.

Hughes, James Mercer Langston (1901–1967) Ancestors. WikiTree. https://www.wikitree.com/wiki/Hughes-28.

Illinois State University, Traditions. *The Story of "Normal." Illinois State Normal University, Est. 1857* (March 29, 2024) https://traditions.illinoisstate.edu/isnu/#:~:text=The%20new%20ISU&text=The%20state%20approved%20the%20change,multipurpose%20developing%20liberal%20arts%20university.

Jefferson, Thomas. "Thomas Jefferson's Attitudes Toward Slavery." Monticello. https://www.monticello.org/research-education/thomas-jefferson-encyclopedia/thomas-Jefferson-s-attitudes-toward-slavery/.

———. "This Deplorable Entanglement." Monticello. https://www.monticello.org/slavery/jefferson-slavery/thomas-jefferson-liberty-slavery/this-deplorable-entanglement/.

Kansas History Web Sites. "Langston Hughes on his racial and ethnic background." http://www.kansashistory.us/hughestext.html.

Kansas State Agricultural College, Information on Graduates. 1867–1913. "1876 (Sawyer) Kedzie Jones, Nellie" and "1897 (Vandivert) Remick, Harriet Agnes" (1914). https://www.ksgenweb.org/education/ksu/ksugrads1.html.

Karmel, Marjorie. *Thank You, Dr. Lamaze*. Philadelphia: Lippincott, 1965. Doubleday (1959).

Kellett, Carol. *Legacy of Leadership: Human Ecology at Kansas State University*. Kansas State University College of Human Ecology (2010) 8–11. https://www.hhs.k-state.edu/archive/legacy-of-leadership.pdf.

Kennedy, John F. Presidential Library and Museum. "Moon Shot – JFK and Space Exploration." https://www.jfklibrary.org/visit-museum/exhibits/past-exhibits/moon-shot-jfk-and-space-exploration.

———. "The Peace Corps." https://www.jfklibrary.org/visit-museum/exhibits/permanent-exhibits/the-peace-corps.

Kessler, Leonard and Ruby. Teresa Flora. *Footprints of Sand Creek*. Sawyer, Kansas (2007).

Koppel, Lily. *The Astronaut Wives Club*. New York: Hachette Book, 2013.

Legends of America. "Dust Bowl Days or the 'Dirty Thirties.'" https://www.legendsofamerica.com/20th-dustbowl/.

Lincoln, Abraham. "Second Inaugural Address, March 4, 1865." https://www.abrahamlincolnonline.org/lincoln/speeches/inaug2.htm.

BIBLIOGRAPHY

Marshall, Catherine. *Mr. Jones Meet the Master*. New Jersey: Fleming H. Revell, 1950.

———. *A Man Called Peter*. New York: McGraw-Hill (1951) 3, 222, 235–238.

Massachusetts, U.S., Soldiers and Sailors in the Revolutionary War. "In the War of the Revolution, Jonathan Evans." Vol. 05 (1891) 403.

"Mary Kessler Vandivert." *The Manhattan Republic*. Manhattan, Kansas (January 18, 1906) 1.

"Mary Ursula Kessler." Obituary. *Bethany Republican-Clipper*. Bethany, Missouri (January 25, 1906) 4.

Mead, Frank S. *Handbook of Denominations in the United States*. Nashville: Abingdon. 1983.

Mennonite Church USA. "History." https://www.mennoniteusa.org/who-are-mennonites/history/.

"Mrs. Vandivert Dead." *The Manhattan Republic*. Manhattan, Kansas (January 18, 1906) 5.

Murphy, Kevin. *Remembering Comedian Phyllis Diller: 1917–2012)* (August 24, 2912). https://www.timesnewspapers.com/webster-kirkwoodtimes/features/remembering-comedian-phyllis-diller-1917-2012/article_60989c18-7e3d-5e6e-81ee-2593c0e9fbca.html.

National Archives, Military Records. "DCAS Vietnam Conflict Ext. File Incident Death Date." https://www.archives.gov/research/military/vietnam-war/casualty-statistics

National Air and Space Museum. "Alan Shepard: First American in Space." Smithsonian. https://airandspace.si.edu/explore/stories/alan-shepard.

———. "Racing to Space: Gagarin and Shepard." Smithsonian. https://airandspace.si.edu/explore/stories/gagarin-vs-shepard.

The New Amsterdam History Center (2011) "The Story of New Amsterdam." https://www.newamsterdamhistorycenter.org/bios/origins.html.

"Number of missing in Kerr County remains at 2; at least 135 died in Texas floods." Texas Public Radio, August 11, 2025. https://www.tpr.org/live-updates/kerrville-flooding-texas-hill-country.

Patricia Corrigan Papers. Preliminary Inventory S0867 (SA3851) State Historical Society of Missouri Research Center–St. Louis.

Penn, William. "William Penn: English Quaker Leader and Colonist." https://www.britannica.com/biography/William-Penn-English-Quaker-leader-and-colonist.

Pennsylvania Historical and Museum Committee. "1581–1776: The Quaker Province, The Founding of Pennsylvania." https://www.phmc.state.pa.us/portal/communities/pa-history/1681-1776.html.

Poetry Foundation. "T.S. Eliot (1888–1965)" https://www.poetryfoundation.org/poets/t-s-eliot.

Quarles, Francis. *Emblems* (1635) Princeton; americana. Princeton Theological Seminary Library. New York: N. Tibbals, 1800.

———. *From 'A Feast for Wormes.'* All Poetry. https://allpoetry.com/poem/14374041-From—A-Feast-For-Wormes—by-Francis-Quarles.

———. "Francis Quarles (1592–1644)" Family Tree. https://quarlesfamilytree.com/francis-quarles-1592-1644/#google_vignette

Remick Country Doctor Museum & Farm. Tamworth, New Hampshire. https://newsite.remickmuseum.org/.

Remick, Malvina Patterson. Obituaries. https://images.findagrave.com/photos/2018/38/42844631_1518156546.jpg.

BIBLIOGRAPHY

The Society of Colonial Wars. "The Lexington Alarm, 1775." https://www.colonialwarsct.org/1775_lex_alarm.htm.

Start, Clarissa. "Bewigs of Webster Groves to be Featured Today on Wide Wide World Show." *St. Louis Post-Dispatch*. St. Louis, Missouri (February 16, 1958).

———. "Sixteen in – Where?" *Webster Groves*. The City of Webster Groves (1975) 231–239.

Tarter, Steve. "BU Woman Professor was Pioneer in Home Economics when Bradley started in 1897" (June 3, 2024). https://www/wcbu.org/local-news/2024-06-03/bu-woman-professor-was-pioneer-in-home-economics-when-bradley-started-in-1897.

Taylor, James. "Fire and Rain." Warner Bros. Records, 1970.

Threlfall, John Brooks. *The Ancestry of Thomas Bradbury (1611–1695) and His wife Mary (Perkins) Bradbury (1615–1700) of Salisbury Massachusetts*. Madison: John Brooks Threlfall (1995) 1–4, 561, 566.

United States Holocaust Memorial Museum. "The 20th Armored Division During World War II." Holocaust Encyclopedia. https://encyclopedia.ushmm.org/content/en/article/the-20th-armored-division.

University of London. "The Story Behind Keep Calm and Carry On." 2014. https://www.london.ac.uk/about/history/history-senate-house/story-behind-keep-calm-carry.

The Vindicator Committee. *Doctrinal Treatise, Fifth Edition*. Union City, Ohio (May 1991).

Weigel, Marie. "What a Study Club Meant to Young Manhattan in 1895." 60th Anniversary Luncheon. Keynote Address (February 15, 1955) The Riley County Historical Society and Museum.

Wirtz, Ann Brubaker Greenleaf. "Reverence for Kansas Roots." *The Pratt Tribune*. Pratt, Kansas (November 14, 2008).

———. *Our Lives in Verse, Everyday Poetry*. Bloomington, Indiana: WestBow, 2022.

Wirtz, Ann Greenleaf. *Hand of Mercy, A Story of God's Grace*. Greenville, South Carolina: AE Books, ambassador-international.com (2015) 135–139.

Wolf, Max, Mrs. "One of City's Oldest Meeting Groups is Tuesday Afternoon Club." *Manhattan Mercury*, Centennial Edition (1955) The Riley County Historical Society and Museum.

Wolfe, Tom. *The Right Stuff*. New York: Farrar, Straus and Giroux, 1979.

Wordsworth, William, and Mary Wordsworth. ed. Beth Darlington. *The Love Letters of William and Mary Wordsworth*. Cornell University (April 2, 2009). https://www.cornellpress.cornell.edu/book/9780801475337/the-love-letters-of-william-and-mary-wordsworth/#bookTabs=1.

Yost, Russell. "Richard Warren Family Tree & Descendants." The History Junkie (February 2, 2023). https://thehistoryjunkie.com/richard-warren-family-tree-and-descendants/.

Zunes, Stephen, and Jesse Laird. "The US Anti-Vietnam War Movement (1964–1973). International Center on Nonviolent Conflict (January 2010). https://www.nonviolent-conflict.org/us-anti-vietnam-war-movement-1964-1973/.

www.ingramcontent.com/pod-product-compliance
Lightning Source LLC
Chambersburg PA
CBHW071713160426
43195CB00012B/1663